HUNTING
BLUE:

HUNTING BLUE:
AND HATING AMERICA

RAMA

XULON ELITE

Xulon Press Elite
555 Winderley Pl, Suite 225
Maitland, FL 32751
407.339.4217
www.xulonpress.com

Xulon Elite

© 2024 by RAMA

All rights reserved solely by the author. The author guarantees all contents are original and do not infringe upon the legal rights of any other person or work. No part of this book may be reproduced in any form without the permission of the author.

Due to the changing nature of the Internet, if there are any web addresses, links, or URLs included in this manuscript, these may have been altered and may no longer be accessible. The views and opinions shared in this book belong solely to the author and do not necessarily reflect those of the publisher. The publisher therefore disclaims responsibility for the views or opinions expressed within the work.

Unless otherwise indicated, Scripture quotations taken from the Holy Bible, New International Version (NIV). Copyright © 1973, 1978, 1984, 2011 by Biblica, Inc.™. Used by permission. All rights reserved.

Paperback ISBN-13: 979-8-86850-679-6
Ebook ISBN-13: 979-8-86850-680-2

Contents

Author's Note vii
Prologue. ix
The Donald Trump Story. 1
A Quick Mental Exercise 2
1955 The Emmett Till Story-Money, Mississippi. 2

2012 The Philip Rivers Story-Harvey, Louisiana. 4
2012 The Bleyer, Becker, and Roberts Story-Shreveport, Louisiana. 6
2012 The Trayvon Martin Story-Sanford, Florida. 10
2012 The Pitts Boys Story-Lafayette, Louisiana. 11
2012 The Junior Smythe Story-St. Louis, Missouri. 13
2012 The Barry Cannon Story-Casselberry, Florida 16

2014 A Kindergarten Story-Berkely, Missouri 18
2014 The Michael Brown Story-Ferguson, Missouri. 20
2014 The Blue Lives Matter Story-NYC, Los Angeles 21
2014 The Eric Garner Story-Staten Island, New York 22
2014 The Harold Giles Story-Grand Island, Louisiana 25
2014 The Dwayne and Dwight Jackson Story-Lake Charles, Louisiana. 27

2015 The Freddy Gray Story-Baltimore, Maryland 29
2015 The Peterson/Bozeman Story-Metairie, Louisiana 30
2015 The Baba Cakes Story-Metairie, Louisiana. 32
2015 The Muhigrdin d'Baha Story-New Orleans, Louisiana. 33

2016 The Dominique and Iman Story-Atlanta, Georgia. 35
2016 The Jeremiah Wilson Story-Woodstock, Georgia 37

2016 The Dallas Assassinations-Dallas, Texas 38
2016 The Sandra Brown Story-Mobile, Alabama. 39
2016 The Calvin Dunne Story-Charlotte, North Carolina. 41
2016 The Rooney Porter Story-Orange, Texas 44
2016 The Ronnie Wilcox Story-Slidell, Louisiana 45
2016 The Ryan Winston Story-Tuscaloosa, Alabama 47

2017 The Harold Martin Story-Brady, Texas 48
2017 The Leon Starks Story-Dollywood 50
2017 The Gerald Holland Story-Harvey, Louisiana 53
2017 The Luis Brocamontes Story-Sacramento, California 54
2017 The Rodney Abrams Story-Forest Orchard, Oklahoma 55
2017 The Riley Williams Story-Gretna, Louisiana 57

2018 The Justin Billa Story-Touliminville, Alabama 58
2018 The Chase Maddow Story-Locust Grove, Georgia. 59

2018 The Paul Bauer Story-Chicago, Illinois 60
2018 The Markeith Floyd Story-Orlando, Florida. 60
2018 When Will It All Stop? An Opinion 61
2018 Police Shootings Stats 62
2018 Random Thoughts On Hatred 64

The Tom Dooley and Mack the Knife Stories. 70
Endnotes 73

Author's Note

Much of "Hunting Blue: And Hating America" was written during the Covid years (2019-2022). Certain police stories in the prior two decades were memorable. And, in the two or three years since Covid, many police actions captured the interest of young and old alike. Upon seeing flashing lights of law enforcement, we tend to slow down or even stop to see what we can see.

I grew-up near St. Louis, Missouri, where crime has been a problem for many years. My first five years out of college were spent in Detroit, experiencing the 'long hot summer of '67". The street riots there, mainly confrontations of black residents with DPD, resulted in 43 deaths, 342 injuries, and 14,000 buildings burned to the ground. 7,000 National Guard and U.S. Army troops were called to service.[1] There was a race riot in Detroit in 1943; the 1967 variety more violent. I've lived in New York City and, on two occasions, in New Orleans.

My first subway trip was to complete some business for my school in Queens. I sat across from two Latino youths, who watched me and flashed double edge razors on their tongues, changing from one cheek to the other. Somehow I managed my safety on that thrilling ride and others into Brooklyn or other parts of the city.

We lived in an apartment on Cooper Avenue. A young kid occasionally shot into our windows from his window across the street. When we complained, the mother said, "Well, it's only a BB gun."

In New Orleans, my son's best friend in high school was shot and killed by a black youth. Neill was the son of our best friends, the Stricklands.

In south Florida, my wife, young daughter, and I rented for a short while from a dentist in town. Their were separate entrances to the office and separate drinking fountains (early '70s).

As I write this author's note, the report in Chicago for the Fourth of July weekend indicated that one hundred people were shot, seventeen killed. We hear about Chicago a lot but such violence is reported elsewhere regularly.[2]

I liked reading a newspaper. But I stopped the Times Picayune paper a decade ago, both because of the front pages always about the hatred in the city, and the liberal slant of the editors. For the most part, I don't tune-in to the local news. It's just not very pleasant! St. Louis and New Orleans seem to always be in the top five cities on reported murders.

My driving record is quite good, though "the police" have written several traffic citations on me. On one trip from the Big Apple to the Big Easy, on an Easter Sunday morning, a patrolman stopped me, doing 80 in a 55. The officer was not happy with me. But I've never been confrontational or disrespectful with police.

Communities need law and order. The "defund the police" people in much of our country have been part of the problem. District attorneys, liberal judges, and mayors have betrayed us with soft-on-crime policies, certainly factors in the writing of these books. I proudly BACK THE BLUE!

Prologue

Mark Lavin, an American news analyst, columnist, lawyer, political commentator, writer, and radio/TV personality, published "The Democrat Party Hates America." Lavin believes, and I think, proves, that Democrat hatred has ben obvious for at least the last century, and maybe since the late 1800s. The disrespect for law enforcement today is hate at its best. There seems to be a lot of Democrats who are unhappy, bitter, angry, and spiteful folks.

I'm not a history buff! But I suspect that at the founding of our republic, there were unhappy, hateful people too? Two hundred and fifty years later, hatred in America has not abated.

The moment Donald Trump announced his candidacy for the highest office in our land, many found him hard to love. But his "Make America Great Again" theme resonated quickly. He accomplished many of his goals and then Covid sidetracked all of us.

I do a lot of thinking while trying to fall asleep. The more I considered my new subtitle, Biblical thoughts came to mind. The Scriptural account of Cain and Abel (Genesis 4), and that sibling rivalry, fir perfectly into the hatred theme.

Genesis 4:2 "Abel was a keeper of sheep' Cain a tiller of the ground," both farmers of a sort. Verse 3: "in the process of time, Cain brought an offering of the fruit of the ground to the Lord." Abel's offering: "of the first born of his flock and of their fat." We don't know the specifics, but the Bible tells us that the Lord respected Abel's offering but did not respect Cain's.

I did not check any related bible texts (Leviticus, Numbers, Hebrews), leaving my undergrad Kretzman's Bible Commentary on the dusty bookshelf. But it sounds like jealousey to me? Verse5: "And Cain was very angry, and his countenance fell." Premeditation?

Interesting! Verse 8: "And Cain talked with his brother." That conversation (maybe, better said confrontation) apparently did not go well. When the two were in the field, "Cain rose up against Abel his brother and killed him." You can read the rest of the story in vv 9-16.

What do you think? Any of that anger, hatred, jealousy, and violence happening in the USA today?

On a lighter side, and a bit of a tangent, does the name Rod Smart ring a bell with you? Tarrold DeShawn Rod Smart played football with the Western Kentucky Hilltoppers, was signed by the San Diego Chargers in 2000, an undrafted free agent, ultimately released prior to the start of that NFL season. He caught on with the XFL Las Vegas Outlaws, a league that had far less restrictive rules about the game. Players were allowed to choose their own identity for the back of their jersey. Smart chose "He Hate Me" for his jersey (the most sold jersey of the XFL). Serious football fans remember Smart's nickname, jersey, and game stats on the gridiron.[3]

Smart played with the Carolina Panthers (2002-2005) and did well in various offensive positions as he had done in college football. The "He Hate Me" name resulted in a good bit of notoriety. Stories of hatred and animosity have always outsold stories of love and compassion.

This book is not a happy read for a restful weekend at the beach. The non-fiction parts relate some of the police arrests and killing or injury of well-known offenders of the law: Michael Brown in Ferguson, Missouri, Alton Sterling in Baton Rouge, Louisiana, Eric Garner in NYC, Freddie Gray in Baltimore, Maryland. George Floyd in Minneapolis, Jacob Blake in Kenosha, and Briana Taylor in Louisville. You might want to research each FYI?

I hope Your reading results in a better understanding and appreciation for law and order in American culture of the mid-2020s. You might wonder if some of the stories are just fiction?

Sneaky? Okay, maybe. It was part of my thinking from the start.

Lastly, the hatred and disrespect for law and order, rejuvenated by our immigration policies since 2020, has only gotten worse. Local and national violent crime committed by illegals in reported every week, New York City a prime example, in early 2024. Added to an already angered, divided, and hateful society, it makes it difficult to stop writing the stories. They just keep on coming.

As a result, "Hunting Blue: and Hating America" has developed into two books. The first of two includes a true story from 1955 and stories through 2018. The second book, subtitle "The Hatred Continues," stories through 2024. I hope you'll purchase both.

The Donald Trump Story

NOT EVERYONE WILL remember stories about Emmett Till, Trayvon Martin, Luis Broncamontes, the Dallas assassinations (five police officers ambushed and killed), and others in these two books. At least, the details about those will be quite fuzzy for most readers. But nearly everyone remembers the Butler Pennsylvania assassination attempt on former president Donald Trump, July, 2024.

In addition to injuring the former president, three other men were shot. Corey Comperatore died of his wounds. David Dutch and James Copenhaver were hit by one or more bullets but recovered from the wounds.

The shooter was killed by a USSS sniper, assigned to the rally. The Director of the USSS ultimately resigned her office, ineptitude and incompetence her legacy. Our FBI Director was roundly criticized for the "answers" he gave to a congressional committee, weeks after the rally.

Just one hundred days from the Presidential election, Donald Trump continued to hold rallies in many states following an excellent Republican National Convention in Milwaukee. The Democrat National Convention in Chicago was held two weeks hence, their presidential candidate still undecided after Joe Biden was forced to bow-out of his campaign yet apparently allowed to finish his term, his competence and abilities questioned by many. So, the Donald Trump story may not be a short story? One hundred days from the election, Trump held a lead, though slight, in most battle ground states.

Why two books? When was the last time you purchased a six hundred page paperback? Two three hundred page paperbacks are much more attractive for sales. It also help me with financing the two publications. The titles of the books look similar; the subtitles different. That by publishers request so as not to cause confusion when ordered at bookstores or on-line.

A Quick Mental Exercise

MAKE TWO LISTS: one, name the people you love; two, name the people you hate (dislike, loothe, dispise, detest). Use real names. Take this seriously. Rank them.

Your first list might be lengthy, so limit it to top five if you can. I'm guessing your second list might not be long. So limit it to five. If you cannot think of one person you hate, God bless you. May it always be so!

Stories for "Hunting Blue" were written mostly in the Covid years. I had lots of time on my hands. The original subtitle for the book (s) was "In the Line of Duty." I changed the subtitle to "And Hating America." You'll recognize some subthemes and perhaps some political bias, especially in the fictional stories.

Hatred has been part of society since the beginning. Hatred of law enforcement is a more recent matter. The 2016 election of Donald Trump and defeat of Hillary Clinton caused hatred to abound. Progressives in America have never accepted the 2016 national electoral voice. That political hatred will, no doubt, continue through 2024 and beyond.

* * *

The Emmett Till Story

AN AFRICAN-AMERICAN TEEN, Emmett Luis Till, visited relatives in the Mississippi Delta town of Money. Fourteen, and from Chicago, perhaps unfamiliar with the Jim Crow era in the south, reportedly Till flirted with a white woman in a grocery store.

The Jim Crow historical period lasted into the 1960s, having begun nearly a century earlier. The story details are somewhat disputed. The woman was Carolyn Bryant.

Carolyn's husband and half-brother found Till, dragged him from an uncle's house, and lynched him, after beating and mutilating him, and shooting him in the head. His body was then sunk in a nearby river, the Talahatchie. Later discovered, the family held an open-casket funeral and properly buried him.

Bryant's husband and accomplice were acquitted by an all-white jury. Emmett Till became an icon of the Civil Rights movement in the USA in the "separate but equal" segregation years in America.

In March of 2012, the Department of Justice sent a report to Congress saying that new evidence had been discovered and the Till case was reopened.[4]

In 2017, Timothy Tyson, a senior researcher at Duke University, published a book on the murder, "The Blood of Emmett Till." In the book, some statements of Carolyn Bryant were restated, changing some of what actually happened in the grocery store.

In July of 2018, Jarvis DeBerry, a liberal writer for the Times-Picayune in New Orleans, commented in an article saying, "It's too late to make-up for Emmett Till's murder." Among other things supporting Till's family, and remembering his death, DeBerry continued, " I don't know what it's like for black boys born in Mississippi today. I don't know if Till's lynching holds any meaning for them. But for me, his sory is a reminder on my vulnerability, a reminder that black boys like me had been and could be slandered, snatched, mangled, and murdered; their killers allowed to strut around a free men."[5]

Roy Bryant, Carolyn's husband, died at the age of 63. J. W. Milam died at 61. The two were not regarded well by many in Mississippi after their acquittal.

Timothy Tyson was interviewed by NPR. He stated, "I think that it's a cynical political charade and utter hypocrisy for the Justice Department of Jeff Beauregard Sessions and Donald Trump to begin caring about a black child murdered in 1955 when they're holding children of color in cages"… etc., etc., etc." That referenced the loud cry about the Trump administration's handling of immigration of illegals at the southern border."

3

Tyson went on to write, "Jeff Sessions has spent his whole career supporting restrictions on voting rights. And I think it's rich with irony".[6]

Two sides to the story? More conservative writers and reporters were quick to correct the "cages" reference, saying that such "holding" circumstances were thanks to the Obama administration. You could still hear the "children in cages" falsehood twenty years later in a Trump context.

National Public Radio was established by an act of congress more than fifty years ago (2-26-70). NPR has offices in California and Washington D. C. NPR's listeners are mostly higher educated white, some republican, some democrat, and some independents. A 2019 survey found that their audience today might be as much as ninety percent Democrat.[7]

* * *

The Philip Rivers Story

THE HURRICANE SEASON in the Gulf South and southeastern USA begins June 1 and extends through the end of November. Storms come off the west coast of Africa, travel across the Atlantic, directed by various winds and water conditions. Some storms develop into tropical systems, perhaps actual hurricanes (wind speeds starting at 75 miles per hour, the big and memorable ones as much as 130 or more miles per hour). The storms may strike lands in the Caribbean, some go into central America and Mexico, travel to Texas, or make land fall anywhere on Gulf shores. The folks who live in East Texas, Louisiana, Mississippi, Alabama, and the west coast of Florida are always happy to see the systems turn north and travel up the Atlantic coast.

The hurricane season is the wet or rainy season in the deep south. The New Orleans area receives, on average, 62+ inches of precipitation yearly, the month of July usually the wettest.

Stacy Simmons was attending a police training, sometimes called an academy, and had nearly completed requirements for joining the police department of Jefferson Parish, just west of New Orleans. She had dropped-off her two children at the local public school in Gretna, and was excited about finishing the training with three dozen others wanting a career in law enforcement. She had stopped at a Walmart in Harvey to buy cat food for Ginger and the Captain, her two cats who spoke to her upon leaving the house. Temptation treats, especially the dairy and chicken flavors were faves.

A hard shower overnight had left puddles on the parking lot, causing her to take a circuitous route to her car, unfortunately parked in a shallow puddle. But she had wet shoes often, a native of Westwego, Louisiana.

A large, black Chevy Tahoe SUV with no license plate was parked across from Stacy, the engine running. The only other vehicle, somewhat of a clunker, was a small Toyota, gun metal gray. The Tercell started to bac-up, causing her to stop and wait. She jumped to a yellow curb o avoid the vehicle. The two vehicles seemed a bit strange, "vehicles of interest" maybe, so she watched them for a moment. The police academy was less than five minutes from the store, located at the Harry Lee Law Enforcement Complex on the Westbank Expressway.

Stacy could not see anyone but the driver in the SUV, the windows darkly tinted. She felt the same about the small Toyota. She opened a granola snack bar and sipped a still hot coffee, her usual morning repast. It was just after 8:00 AM, many night shift workers just leaving the store.

Philip Rivers, a new employee at the Walmart, called his wife to ask if she needed anything at the house. He worked a three-hour, part-time job as a security cop, 5:00-8:00, four days a week. A retired policeman from the Orleans Parish Police Department, there had never been a problem in his first six weeks at the store. He expected no problems today.

Philip parked his new Camry nearly fifty yards from the store entrance, almost to the McDonalds on Manhattan Blvd. Many mornings he'd get a biscuit or two and two burritos to share with his wife, Wilma, while they watched a little cable news. This would not be a good news day.

Halfway to his car, the Toyota screeched toward Rivers, splashing water to both sides. Rivers turned to see what was happening behind him and was struck hard, knocking him to the wet lot. The hooded driver ran to the SUV following, now only a half mile from the I-10 service road, their escape route, either east or west.

Rivers dies at the scene with spinal cord and head injuries.

Witnesses were few because of a light rain that had started. Both vehicles were discovered to have been stolen from a Midas muffler shop on Chef Menteur Highway. Jefferson Parish investigators found no evidence in either car to help with their investigation.

Stacy Simmons had not seen what was called a vehicular manslaughter death. Her description of the two cars were the same as reported by those in the fast food line, the one hooded man only visible for an instant and the SUV driver never seen. She did offer her instincts to the investigating officers, arriving late for her last day of training. He promised himself to wear a police uniform with pride every day, committed to a law enforcement career.

Wilma had no family to console her. After the house sold, Stacy and her two young boys helped her to move to an assisted living facility in Mobile.

* * *

The Bleyer, Becker, and Roberts Story

Byrd High School in Shreveport, Louisiana, BFFs galore, mostly Freshman girls who couldn't believe that they were part of a very large secondary school. They would be the graduating class of 2016, the next four years filled with youthful memories.

Albert Bleyer, Ron Becker, and Will Roberts had that "best friends" relationship already in Sixth Grade at Caddo Parish Middle Magnet

School, also a sizeable population of twelve hundred-plus students. The three loved wave boarding, hunting, and rap music; Drake their favorite.

Much of the threesome's time out of school was spent cruising in Al's Jeep Wrangler, drinking a few cold ones on the sly, and sometimes triple dating for a movie, dinner, and hanging-out at one of the girls' houses. All three families were quite well-to-do, so par-time jobs were not a priority for the boys or for their parents.

Shreveport, tucked into the northwestern part of the state, is the home of LSU-Shreveport, Centenary College, and southern University of Shreveport. The three choose to spend their college years at Centenary, a 4-year liberal arts college, established with Methodist affiliation in 1825. Like many, each had some idea of future careers, but none was anxious to rush that decision. Some parents and/or grandparents pushed them toward education, others to medicine or dentistry. One of Will's uncles thought the three should pursue law enforcement, maybe the state patrol? The three had regular contests of physical strength, no one in particular being the all-around best.

In Biology 101, the only class the three attended together, in their first semester, Dr. Ed Lueck took a liking to the three and they to him. Dr. Lueck was well-known on campus for planting and caring for more than two hundred native trees and shrubs among the hilly landscape of Centenary. Students in his classes were often required to learn many of the species, identifying them by their leaves, bark, or structure.

The guys soon had somewhat steady girls, all fellow students, all Texans. Just before the Mardi Gras season in March, the three girlfriends walked to their dorms late in the evening. They took the path that went through the arboretum, Dr. Lueck's doing, a scarry place with little light, many trees not yet leafed-out for spring and summer.

A group of young teens, the girls described them as a gang, confronted the girls five minutes from the safety of their dormitory. Their screams attracted the attention of the Department of Public Safety officer who doubled as a campus policeman. The DPS building was not a part of Centenary but was immediately next door. Two of the gang were apprehended within minutes of the scare, all six of the group younger than sixteen. The two brought to the DPS office for identification and parent-pickup told the authorities the confrontation was part of an initiation into a local gang called the Shreveport Taxi.

No weapons were found among the Taxi hopefuls. All six were advised never to be on campus again, such to be noted as part of juvey records in the city.

The LSU-Shreveport campus is twenty minutes from Centenary, the LSU soccer team being housed there. Centenary teams play and compete in NCAA Division III, chiefly swimming, baseball, and soccer. The Blyer, Becker, and Roberts names were not part of any athletic roster. They did too much fishing, hunting, and water skiing to be serious swimmers or ball players. Four or more years of college life would quickly fly by. They had better things to do than to be on the practice field and team bus all the time.

Becker was the real ladies' man. He and Maria Villar were headed to the altar before graduation, a baby due in late summer. The expected child caused a bit of a problem because Blyer and Roberts still wanted to go to local haunts with him. Maria, and more importantly, her father, told Ron his carousing days had ended and that he needed to get a job if he was to be a responsible young dad. His two buddies still frequented the Strangebrew bar, especially on Thursday night when you could get $1.00 beers in any size cup you brought with you. When Ronnie wasn't working, the three, and often, the six, still met at the Rhino Coffee Shop or El Comps, the abbreviated name for their favorite Mexican eatery, El Compadre.

Another popular meeting place for the young men was a local soft-serve ice cream joint.

More and more the guys' career directions centered on law enforcement. They took classes in psychology, sociology, and human behavior that might help them if they were serious about becoming policemen. Ronnie had his eyes on a position with the DPS especially if Maria finished her degree at Centenary. Mr. Mrs. Villar were on board with the plans of the happy couple.

Employment with DPS and with local police departments (Bossier City, Ruston, and Texarkana) varied a bit. By March of 2016, all three had met the requirements of becoming policemen, Ron at the DPS in Shreveport, and Al and Will in Bossier City.

Requirements for becoming policemen in Louisiana cities included a high school diploma, the age of 20 or 21, good physical and psychological condition, a valid driver's license, and a good driving record.

Entry level salaries for policemen in New Orleans might be $40,000.00. The highest paid perhaps $130,000.00. In smaller communities like Shreveport, though it was the third largest city in the state, might be as much as $7,000.00 less. You could be paid about $3,000.00 while attending a police adademy. Your uniform and equipment were provided.

Just prior to Halloween, Blyer, Becker, and Roberts enjoyed a rare late afternoon treat at a Dairy Queen. Having made the ice cream stop many times before they worked regular shifts, everyone had their favorite: the peanut buster parfait for Al, a banana split for Ron, and a hot fudge sundae for Will. They shared their recent police activities. Ron was an obvious proud father, Marita now six month old.

Blyer and Roberts left their patrol cars, off-duty guys at times allowed to drive home in them. Blyer went back to the store after a group hug to get a couple of Dilly Bars which Maria liked o give her infant, one-half at a time. He bought a couple for Maria as well, living just a few blocks from the DQ.

Officer Ron Becker we killed that early evening in the store parking lot, two deadly shots from an A-400 Extreme, Baretta pistol.

Witnesses reported a black youth speeding away on what one of them thought was a Kawasaki cycle, maybe a Ninja 600, a lot of chrome and mostly sky blue. The shooter was never apprehended.

A Maria-Marita Go-Fund-Me account was arranged by officers Blyer and Roberts, assisted by faculty and friends of Centenary College. Dilly bars were provided by Dairy Queen whenever the Beckers family wanted more. Mostly now though, the mom and baby ordered Ronnie's favorite banana split, always gratis.

The Trayvon Martin Story– Sanford, Florida[8]

WHEN DID IT all start? Some say it began with Trayvon Martin. Others say much earlier. Some say way back in American history.

Trayvon Martin was the 17-year-old, shot and killed by George Zimmerman, a 28-year-old neighborhood security guard. Martin was black. Zimmerman was of mixed ancestry. Many recall Barak Obama's comment about the case, "Trayvon could have been my boy." Perhaps a poor choice of words?

There was an altercation between Martin and Zimmerman. The security guard was injured. The Florida youth died!

Charged with murder, Zimmerman pleaded self-defense. He was ultimately acquitted. The Department of Justice reviewed the case as a civil right matter. Zimmerman was not charged; insufficient evidence.

Between August, 2014, and July, 2017, there were four events where black men were injured or killed by police officers, each receiving national attention and public outcry. Law enforcement individuals were accused of acting too quickly, taking action without cause, beatings and brutality that were not justified. These are reported and updated among the fictitious stories that follow.

You might expect police actions and resulting protests in the large cities of our country. But violence became a rural and small-town occurrence as well.

The word used a lot for small towns is "quaint." Talk with those who travel our country and visit such locations, and "unique" is also used in that context: Beaufort, South Carolina, a quaint Low country small town. Carmel-by-the-Sea, California, where you need a permit to wear high heels. Rhinebeck, New York, where you'll find the oldest operating inn. Mystic, Connecticut boasts the largest maritime museum. Dahlonega, Georgia tells all visitors it's where the first major gold rush happened. You can see and shop the largest Christmas store in Frankenmuth, Michigan.

Meadville, Mississippi, a half-hour drive from Natchez, Brookhaven, and McComb has a small-town history too. In May, 1964, two young African-American men were abducted as they hitchhiked in the state. The bodies of Charles Moore, a student of Alcorn State College, and Henry Hezekiah Die, a millworker friend, were tortured and killed by the Ku Klux Klan, bodies found two months later. Moore and Dee were transported across the state, tied to farm equipment, and dropped into the Mississippi River.[9]

Two individuals were arrested, but the District Attorney eventually dropped charges against them; insufficient evidence to go to trial. A wave of violent protests followed, six related killings as a matter of record.

* * *

The Pitts Boys Story– Lafayette, Louisiana

WOMEN'S HOSPITAL, LAFAYETTE, Louisiana, just after midnight, fraternal twins delivered to nineteen-year-old Lakendra Pitts, who had been incarcerated at the Louisiana Correctional Institute for Women, in Gabriel, near Gonzalez, Louisiana. Lakendra was transferred to Lafayette to give birth. Her relatives nearby were dealing with her sale of heroin charges, now on hold. Her grandmother and Aunt Willie offered help, and a possible planned childhood for the two boys without the presence of drugs, guns, and parental abuse.

The father of the boys, Rolando Jefferson, wanted no part in raising children. While she had two weeks to decide their future, and breast feeding was difficult, Lakendra angrily shouted to the nurses: "I don't want those kids! Take them away!" Both boys weighed-in at five pounds, one ounce at birth. Their names would be determined by grandma and Aunt Willie.

The first born was named Orlando, for no particular reason. The second, Ohreo, was named for the "Pet of the Week" in the Daily Advertiser, a Gannett newspaper, which served many localities in Acadiana Parish. The pet was a black-and-white Boston Terrier.

Aunt Willie was physically incapacitated in a automobile accident near Carencro. So after six years of doing what they could, Orlando and Ohreo were placed with the Thompson foster care family in Thibideaux. Donald Thompson had been manager of three Walgreen stores and had recently retired. Virginia Thompson, also retired, had been a pediatric nurse for thirty years. Their three children had all flown the coup, and were beginning successful lives, two in Texas, and the other in Houma, Louisiana, a Walgreen manager in training.

Elementary education did not go well. Behavioral records in Middle School and high school result in special school placement and eventually assigned to a second foster home. At the age of eighteen, Orlando and Ohreo escaped the foster fiasco and were seen at a gas station video camera near Shreveport, perhaps headed to Texas or Arkansas? Their bright yellow and black Jeep Wrangler was stolen from a Sonic fast-food lot in Scott, Louisiana. The boys had not seen their mother since the hospital release.

Rolando Jefferson was released from the B. B. Rayburn Correctional Center in Washington Parish after twelve years. He received three citations for DUI in Benton, Arkansas. Numerous sexual assault charges had been filed in Arkansas, none of which resulted in jail time. One such charge was still pending. The Little Rock Police Department reported his demise, which happened in a civil dispute south of the state capital, involving three men at a bar. All with handguns.

Ohreo renamed Orlando, Dizzy, a reference to Disney World. Ohreo never won a spelling bee. His new name, compliments of Dizzy, was Cookie. The two had places to go. With an Obama mindset to totally transform their lives, and maybe America, they'd make their own societal changes.

Dizzy and Cookie despised authority and always saw themselves as victims. Others had a parent or two. Others had nice clothes, better food, opportunities to make it in life. Policemen looked at them warily. The judicial system treated them like property. Theft was part of their daily existence. They's take what they needed, believing that it was owed.

Kenny Roman, their last foster parent, helped them get driver's licenses. He even provided a car, clunker that it was. Soon they'd need other "must haves." They needed reliable transportation, credit cards, a place to stay. And each wanted a gun, often available on the street for personal protection. They had some hunting in mind. But the two were not wildlife enthusiasts.

Orlando Pitts and Ohreo Pitts came into the world just minutes apart. At the age of twenty-six, the Pitts boys left the world, also minutes apart. A three-car accident on I-10 near Katy, Texas, resulted in instant death for Dizz. Cookie died before getting to Hermann Memorial in Katy. Police records indicated that Dizzy was at fault in the "accident." One small child also never recovered from injuries.

The Texas State Police advised officials in Lafayette, Louisiana and in Houma about the deaths. There was no coverage of the Pitts boys in radio, television, or newspaper outlets.

***

The Junior Smythe Story

HALLOWEEN PRACTICES HAVE changed over the years. Though many children in most neighborhoods still dress in costume and go house to house collecting treats, some churches have gone to a trunk-or-treat stop for the fall fun and fare.

In recent years, communities with respectable zoos hold a Boo at the Zoo evening, encouraging parents and their youngsters to spend Halloween at the zoo, plenty of treats handed-out at various stations. In St. Louis, that event had been well-attended for a decade, and plans for the event in 2020 and future years were bigger and better than ever.

Junior Smythe, twenty, would be a part of the fun, but he had ulterior motives. He would not carry a plastic pumpkin to collect treats. He'd go as a chainsaw murderer, a ghostly white mask of the Scarry Movie kind, his cover for a plan that was deadly serious. He practiced his walk-with-a-limp, dragging one leg on the ground. His hasty exit from the zoo would be a sprint to a waiting Kawasaki 2400 ABS.

Junior was angry at his mom, always bitching at him as being lazy as his father. He was angry at his father, in jail at the time for physical assault on the wife. Betty Smythe had just one voice, a yell that was disguised by a scratchy throat resultant from her three packs a day habit with Marlborough. Junior was angry with himself!

Two previous attempts to strike-out at policemen had been foiled. The first was a weather matter in the city near Busch Stadium. The second never happened when other law enforcement arrived just seconds before his intended hit with whom he had numerous run-ins. Lots of planning went into the "third time the charm" effort against a white-haired and mustacheoed policeman who had put his father in jail for spousal abuse.

Jason McKnight was sixty-nine, two children, both with their own growing families and living in the Missouri bootheel. Janis, his wife, was as attractive as any senior citizen he had ever seen. Smythe wondered why some people seemed to have it all and others had such a lesser lot in life.

Officer McKnight coached youth baseball until he turned sixty, the Under 12 kids, most of whom would still listen to an adult training. Jason and Janis both taught Sunday School and volunteered at their local playground on weekends. Before joining the police department in 1967, he taught U.S. History in high school and assisted with the football team. He loved his teaching job as much as his work with the department.

The McKnights always went to Boo at the Zoo, Janis's mother, eighty-eight, in a wheelchair whenever out. She was as fragile as the Venue flytrap, African violets, and maidenhair ferns in the McKnight backyard gardens.

A long line of carved pumpkins was exhibited just outside the gates of the zoo. Local elementary schools held contests and one or two jack-o-lanterns from each school were entered for the final voting for best. Ten winners would receive free zoo passes for the new year.

The McKnights entered after voting for the best carved pumpkin and waited for grandmother who took a restroom break. This was the time to strike. The masked chainsaw killer, the saw obviously a plastic kid's toy, limped-up next to the officer. When the killer got real close, two shots were fired into the upper body. McKnight fell to the sidewalk.

Junior walked hurriedly to the parking lot without any limp. The quick pistol shots mixed with loud music on one side and loud speaker directions on the other, telling those entering how to make the most of their visit at the zoo.

Stunned witnesses provided little helpful information to the investigating park team. McKnight was discovered by a restroom attendant; congealing blood coloring the cold, still green, grass. The EMT crew arrived at the hospital, the officer was already dead.

There had been attempted police assassinations in the St. Louis area ever since the Michael Brown incident in Ferguson, a suburb of St. Louis. Seven police officers had been severely injured in the line of duty in Richmond Heights, Webster Groves, and Jennings; three of them never recovering from their injuries.

The Boo at the Zoo producers and planners announced the next morning on local news that no adult Halloween costumes for future events would be allowed. Many in the Gateway City were thankful for that change. Yet they believed that hatred for law enforcement personnel would continue in St. Louis, always in the top five cities for murder per capita.

The Barry Cannon Story

LANI AND BARRY Cannon had a happy family; good friends, good jobs, and great times in the central Florida community of Sanford, a city of just over 60,000 in Seminole County. Their two children, Kelly, turning eleven at the end of the month and a future volleyball star, and six-year-old Ronnie, who loved baseball and soccer. Barry loved his service with the police department. He spent as much time with each of the kids when off duty.

Jamie Lamb was Lani's best friend, each of them an RN at Lake Mary Hospital. The Lambs were expecting their second child in June. Jackie, in Third Grade, thought she might follow mom's choice of careers.

Barry Cannon and Sonny Lamb had completed a police training in Maitland, Florida, five years earlier. The two were regarded as competent veterans by their superiors and fellow officers.

On vacation for a week, Barry was attempting to close of a new and larger house in Lake Mary, and on this Monday afternoon, had pick-up duty at school.

"Hey, Lani."

"Where are you?"

"Waiting for the kids. 3:15 right?"

"They should be there any minutes. I called Maarta to tell her that you'd be getting the kids all week."

"Wanna go to the park for a half hour? I promised Ronnie we could do that today. I know the Lambs are coming for a late dinner, but we'll have time for some trapping and passing drills with the soccer ball. Bring stuff for Kelly too."

"I got the steaks and veggies for us. The kids can do burgers, okay?"

"Yeah. I'm liking this week away from work. Things are getting real hairy at the department."

"That Martin incident was a real tragedy. Everyone is talking about it at the hospital."

"Sonny said that people are doing more than just talking about it. I'll fill you in on the protests later."

"You needed a break dear. I've enjoyed having you home. Did you play well today?"

"Only played nine holes. But 40 strokes is my best half-round yet. I could get used to this."

"See you at the park."

"Don't forget the frisbees, okay?"

"Ten minutes. Bye."

Kelly and Ronnie had no pets. Their only animals were the stuffed variety. And, like most middle class American families, the kids hardly had room for even one more dog, cat, chipmonk, or Teddy bear. The Tigers and Koalas were supplied by both sets of grandparents at birthday parties and Christmas, one in Virginia and one in Tennessee.

Lani arrived at the park just as her phone rang. It was not Barry. Marta, one of the chiefs at the school after-care program, had called, hung-up, and called again, but left no message.

"Marta, what's up? I'm at the park waiting for Barry and the kids."

"Lani, … the kids are … They are not with Barry. They're with me."

The wife of a police officer took calls from the department, from Barry at times, or from staff or other officers. Rarely were such calls urgent or unusual. Phone calls from school were less frequent, but Marta Thompson was a close friend of the family too. Her hesitant and obviously shaken voice told Lani this call was urgent. This call was bad!

"Lani, get to school fast. Get here now! There's been a shooting!"

Lani's first thought was a school shooting, like the others of recent reporting. A stranger on school grounds, one or more guns, chaos in school hallways and in the parking lot.

"Are the kids okay? Anyone hurt? Where's Barry?"

Marta hung-up on her friend. She knew no details of the sidewalk shooting. Only that a man had been shot and was on the ground.

What seemed like a long thirty minutes was less than half the time to get to McKinley Elementary. The half dozen police cars, the ambulance just arriving, and general huddling of parents and other on-lookers, all appeared gathered near a new Silverado Crewcab, one just purchased by the Cannons. Already cardoned-off with yellow and black tape, EMTs rushing to the scene with a stretcher.

Marta caught Lani as she tried to run under the police tape.

"Lani! Stop! Barry has been shot. Please, stay here with me. I'm here for you."

The blank faces on the other officers and the crowd of parents and school staff told the story. The police chief allowed Lani to stand at the ambulance as Barry was wheeled over. She and Marta accompanied the ambulance to the ER, twenty minutes across town.

Lani's cries were silent, tears of both moms falling like Florida showers. Both women knew, without question or ME report, that the school now had another single mom.

Sgt. Barry Cannon dies at the scene, in the line of duty. This "duty" being that of a loving dad, some hoped for exercise with the family, and dinner with the Lambs.

NOTE:
The Trayvon Martin story is part of this book, happening in Sanford, Florida. The Martin story was the impetus for the Black Lives Matter movement, starting in 2013.

*** * ***

A Kindergarten Story

THE KINDERGARTEN CLASS at Westwood Early Childhood Center, Berkeley, Missouri, arrives for class, a few five-year-olds still not happy to leave mom, dad, or both as they go off to work. The fifteen students were in their first week of school. The teacher, Miss Thompson, and the aide, Sandy Weston, know all the names and have learned much about the parents. After the welcome and allowance for some free play, all seventeen assemble on the center rug for the first lesson of the day.

Miss Thompson: "Boys and girls, this week we are learning about our community helpers. Can anyone tell me what a community is?"

After a brief silence, Kate raises her hand confidently.

Kate: "It's ... uh ...where my mom works. She works at a bank."

Miss Thompson: "Good Kate. That's a good start. Someone else? What is a community? Robbie?"

Robbie: Well, it's ... where we go to school."

Like Ralphie in the "Christmas Story" movie, Robbie is pretty sure his teacher likes his answer.

Miss Thompson: "Right. We call our community Berkeley. Communities are neighborhoods. Communities are towns, cities, and they have names." Then, "So, who are some of our community helpers?"

No hands immediately. The kids look at each other and around the room. A few are a little sleepy. Then Karli's hand shoots up.

Karli: "Uh ... a community helper could be your mailman."

Miss Thompson: "Good! Other helpers in our community?"

Louis: "The trash guys? The garbage guys? They drive the big trucks."

Miss Thompson: "Sure. What would we do without our trash guys?"

Miss Sandy: "Boys and girls. I think Miss Thompson wants us to think about helpers who might wear a uniform. Not all helpers wear a uniform."

Kenny: "Like policemen! Firemen!"

Both teacher and aide smile at each other and at Kenny, who, not only had a great answer but who stayed standing.

Miss Sandy: "Exactly, Ken. Please sit down again. This week we are going to talk about police. Next week we are going to talk about firefighters."

Miss Thompson: "Now I have another question. Does anyone know what a motto is? I'll spell it for you. Motto: m-o-t-t-o."

Miss Sandy wrote the word on the big board.

Again, no quick responses. Then Karli's twin sister, Kari, proudly shouts, "It's what my mom gets at the coffee shop every morning on the way to school; a mocko."

Miss Thompson: "I think you might be thinking about a macchiato. It's a special kind of coffee; ex presso, I think" as she checks with her aide.

Miss Sandy: "A motto is, well, what a business says they do. Dairy Queen advertises on TV, right? They say, "We're not fast food. We're fan food." Boys and girls, that's their motto."

Miss Thompson: "Police have a motto. The motto of the police is "To serve and protect." Let's all say the police motto together: To serve and protect. To serve and protect. To serve and protect. That's the police job in our community. They serve us. Police protect us." Then, "On Thursday, Billy's mom will be here for Show-and-Tell. Billy's mom is a policewoman.

Some of the class look at Billy, maybe wishing that their mom was a policeman. The class talked about community helpers for another five minutes and moved on to the weather for the day.

* * *

The Michael Brown Story

THREE WEEKS EARLIER in Ferguson, Missouri, just two miles from Berkeley in the northern suburb of St. Louis, a "strong arm" robbery of a convenience store occurred a few minutes after noon.

Eighteen-year-old Michael Brown wrestles with a policeman, still in his car, and two shots from the policeman's gun ring out. Brown and a friend with him start to run away. Then Bown stops and charges the policeman.

A total of twelve shots are fired, including the first two with the officer not yet out of the car.

Darren Wilson, a 28-year-old policeman, kills Michael Brown. Six of the bullets hit Brown in the front of his body as he charged toward the officer.[10]

Brown was black. Wilson was white. And the community of Ferguson and surrounding neighborhoods became a violent, protesting, mob-like story for weeks. Coverage of the shooting was constant, riveting the attention of Americans in communities, large and small. The protesting crowds had their own motto: "Hands up! Don't shoot!"

The truth of the matter was that "Hands up. Don't shoot," never happened.

On November 24, the grand jury on the Brown case, decided not to indict Darren Wilson. On March 4, 2015, the United States Department of Justice cleared Wilson of any civil rights violations, saying that Wilson shot the black youth in self-defense.

Witnesses corroborated Wilson's account. Witnesses who incriminated the policeman were found to be not creditable, some of them not having even been at the site where the shooting occurred.

Kindergarten teachers don't talk about such cases with their five-year-olds. Maybe that's a good lesson for us adults, until all the facts are known!

* * *

The Blue Lives Matter Story

NEW YORK CITY Police Department officers Rafael Ramon and Wenjcan Lieu were killed by gunfire on December 20, 2014, in Brooklyn.

On that day, Blue Lives Matter, NYC, was founded by fellow officers. It was a counter effort to the Black Lives Matter movement of 2013. Opened as a non-profit, it sought to make the killing of law enforcement officers a hate crime. Some states have or are taking legislative action to do the eame.[11]

The stated mission of Blue Lives Matter NYC was to help law enforcement officers and their families during their time of need. Blue Lives Matter members are police officers and members from other state and federal agencies that are dedicated to making a difference. More than three hundred billboards publicized the organization in late 2014.

In September, 2015, Los Angeles police officers took part in a Blue Lives Matter rally in Hollywood, supporting the department at a time when the ambush killings of police officers in cities elsewhere have left authorities across the nation feeling under siege.

※ ※ ※

The Eric Garner Story

POLICE OFFICERS OFTEN must use brute force, lethal weapons, or their own physical strength when apprehending criminals. This is certainly the case when individuals resist arrest.

Though other officers assisted in the arrest of Eric Garner, Officer Daniel Pantaleo pulled Garner to the ground, applying a choke hold. Garner was known by the Staten Island Police Department because of previous charges and his criminal record.

Initially Garner's death was ruled a homicide by the ME, because of the compression of the chest and neck. An ambulance was called while the officers held Garner to the ground. He died at the hospital an hour later, asthma, heart disease, and obesity cited as contributing factors. It was widely reported that Garner spoke while being held to the ground, "I can't breathe!" His words became the mantra of protests, printed on signs and yelled in the streets by those who believed the matter to be police brutality and use of unnecessary force.

A grand jury in the Garner case decided not to indict Officer Pantaleo.

In 2019, the U. S. Department of Justice brought charges under federal civil rights law. In early August, an administrative judge recommended that Pantaleo be terminated from the department. Pantaleo was fired, his pension benefits stripped.

As was the case in other police arrests, demonstrations became national news, particularly in late 2014. In July 2015, an out-of-court settlement paid the Garner family nearly six million dollars (paid by the city of New York).

Author's Note: A related story concerns a former marine (Daniel Penny) who was indicted on murder and/or manslaughter charges in the choke-hold death of a homeless black man (Jordan Neely) on a New York City subway (May 1, 2023). The disposition of this case would not begin until October, 2024, or later.

* * *

The Michael Brown Story

JUST DAYS AFTER his high school graduation and an alternative education program, Michael Brown and a friend, Dorian Johnson, were walking in the middle of Canfield Drive, Ferguson, Missouri. Brown was a large 18-year-old, six feet four inches tall and nearly three hundred pounds. Johnson was four years older, and maybe four years wiser, both black youths looking at an uncertain future. It was August 9, 2014, and Brown would not see August 10.

Officer Darren Wilson of the Ferguson Police Department asked (told) the two to use the sidewalk and not hamper traffic. Saying that they were close to their destination, they stayed in the street. Wilson stopped his patrol car, not taking a "No" for an answer.

Brown, apparently trying to take the officer's gun, Wilson still in the vehicle, got shot in the hand and arm, one of two shots fired in the altercation. Both youths ran, Johnson hiding behind some cars, but Brown turned back and charged Wilson once more. The SIG Sauer P-229 pistol was then shot ten more times. Six of those hit Brown and killed him, two head shots causing instant death.

Police records show that Brown had been at the Ferguson Market and Liquor Store at 1:13 AM the night before. The two were at the store again later in the morning, Brown swiping a package of cigarillos and assaulting (shoving) the clerk.

With the struggle in the street, and many police cars arriving with ambulance and EMTs, a crowd gathered at the scene. Unfortunately, Brown's body lay in the street until taken away four hours later.

"Hands up, don't shoot" became the mantra of the crowd, both the day of the shooting and for weeks that followed. In numerous investigations in Ferguson, there was never any evidence that Brown had been shot with his hands up, pleading not to be shot by the officer. Nightly curfews were ordered in Ferguson.

The St. Louis County prosecutor, Robert McCulloch, was in charge of the initial investigation. On November 24, 2014, he decided not to indict Wilson, saying the officer acted in self-defense.

In the days following the shooting, more than three dozen FBI agents went door-to-door, seeking information from witnesses.

A new prosecutor, Wesley Bell, also found no cause to charge Wilson, years later.

A grand jury took three months to consider witness testimony. While most grand juries complete their review of such circumstances in less than a week, the community awaited the prolonged decision. Again, no indictment because of lack of information to charge.

In March of 2015, the U>S> Department of Justice cleared Wilson of any civil rights violations. Wilson suffered bruises on his face and scratches on his neck. Brown's DNA was found on Wilson"s collar, shirt, and pants.

A wrongful death suit by the Brown family resulted in a settlement of an undisclosed amount. It was later reported that Ferguson's insurance company paid the family 1.5 million dollars.

Officer Wilson resigned from the FPD, without severance benefits. He had earlier worked with the Jennings Police Department. For some reason, perhaps many reasons, the Jennings city council decided to shut down the police department. Wilson apparently had difficulty getting hired by other departments after the Brown shooting.

The Ferguson Police Department chief apologized to the Brown family two months after Brown's death. He later resigned from the police force.

Body cameras became a part of law enforcement by action of the Obama administration, seven million dollars appropriated for such.

*　*　*

The Harold Giles Story

"Sgt. Owens; you see what I see?"

"Just another homicide, Tyler. It happens everywhere these days; big cities, small towns, at the beach, at a shopping mall. Why? Do you see something I don't see?

It was late Saturday night. Sunday morning by the time the forensics team finished. The body had been moved a half-hour before midnight. Investigation at the scene required several hours more. At 3:00 AM the quiet community of Grand Island on a barrier island in the Gulf of Mexico was as calm as the sea breeze. The no-see-ems were thick, hungry, and more than pesty.

Six shots had been fired, all of the 9 millimeter ammo recovered, three at the scene and the other three in the victim's chest; no exit wounds. The victim was taken to the Jefferson Community Health Center. The closest hospitals were in Cut Off, Port Sulphur, or Galiana, further north.

Glock 19 Gen 5 pistols or something similar were suspected. The Gen 5 held fifteen rounds. One witness, Chuck Finley, was questioned near the Hurricane Hole Restaurant on Highway #1. He reported seeing two men, young he thought, hurriedly leaving the scene on small cycles. Chuck drove a 2013 XL 1200 Harley. He said he had another, a 2010 Sportster 1200, which he no longer rode. Owens regarded Finley as knowledgeable. A third bike in his tool shed had recently been sold for $9,000.00, a Sportster 883.

Finley told officers the cycles were definitely HDs, maybe Softail Sport Glides. The mud on them made them look like they had some age. Tyler Songy, new with the police department, but well-respected after just eight months on the job, continued the inquiry with the restaurant owner. He and Sgt. Owens wrote their reports over coffee at an all night Race Track station.

The victim was white, elderly, and by himself, probably surprised by the perps as he got into his small Toyota pickup fishing gear in the back. He was a retiree police officer, in Grand Isle for less than ten days, checking out charter fishing places and summer rentals. He had a dozen tourist brochures in the truck from a Visitor's Center, the Wahoo water-front camp marked with a big X, apparently because of well-kept cabins. The Wahoo had access and launch facilities and rented for less than $100.00; the many others ranging upward to $400.00, in season. The victim was identified as Harold Giles, his driver's license and wallet with several hundred dollars found on the floor of the Toyota.

The attackers wore sweats, dark color, and were headed north, little or no traffic at the late hour on Saturday. There was no confirmation of racial identify, but Finley suspected black teens or early twenties

Grand Isla had a population of about 15,000, but, in the summer fishing season, it grew to 20,000. The population was 96 percent white and less than 3 percent black. Crime stats were not reported for individual communities of this Gulf area, most of them Census Designated Places. As of January 1, 2015m the Giles shooting was still open but a cold case with no news leads.

The Dwayne and Dwight Jackson Story

DWAYNE JACKSON WAS a scoundrel. His twin brother, Dwight, even more a low life. Now twenty years old, both had been incarcerated in juvey facilities for much of their teen years. Their few "friends" even called them scumbags, crooks, and SOBs. Judges referred to them as miscreants and reprobates.

Born in Lake Charles, Louisiana, and having no known relatives of either parent, their mother died at twenty-three, killed by her nineteen-year-old husband who, four days later, took his own life, a Smith and Wesson pistol the tool in the tragic twin killing. No one in Lake Charles cared much about Kajana's passing, even fewer shed tears over Jesse's demise. Both had criminal records.

Wards of the court in southwestern Louisiana, Dwayne and Dwight were surprisingly healthy, having the size and strength to have played on any college football team in the state. If only their childhood and growing-up years had been different. Neither competed high school and a GED seemed to be ridiculous to both. They had no permanent address, drifting from place to place, taking whatever work they could find, mostly with roofing crews, sometimes in custodial maintenance, and, in summer months, with highway or city grass cutting and trimming jobs.

Drifting like the smoke of sugar cane fields in Cajan country, the pair latched onto a cadre of other vagabonds near Washington in St. Landry Parish, six young men sharing one apartment. All were African-American, not yet having found their way in life. It was hard to tell that any was interested in their future. There were some girlfriends, some drug use, and shared pre-owned vehicles. Employment in and around Washington was chiefly agricultural which didn't pay much.

Washington, Louisiana, formerly Popular Grove, had a population of less than one thousand. The town's budget was enhanced by ticketing speedsters, the place know as one of the worst speed traps in the state. The racial mix was about 52 percent Black and 43 percent white, most communities like it having small populations of Native Americans, Asians, and Pacific Islanders.

Other small towns in the area include Unice, Gibbs, and Boscoville, each having some police record of the Jacksons.

Local and national news coverage of the Black Lives Matter group intrigued the Jacksons, and, together with other wayward youths, some as young as ten, attended unannounced yet known get-togethers held at parks or playgrounds on weekends.

Black Lives Matter began in 2013 with the use of the hash tag on social media after the much publicized acquittal of George Zimmerman in the shooting death of Trayvon Martin. Everyone talked about the African-American teen and involvement of law enforcement.

The organization, without any formal hierarchy, became nationally recognized for its street demonstrations following the 2014 deaths of two other well-remembered names: Michael Brown and Eric Garner. BLM participants demonstrated against their deaths and others. They were especially active in the summer of 2015 because of the coming presidential elections.

Originators of the BLM movement, Alicia, Garza, Patrisse Cullors, and Opel Tometi expanded the movement into a national network of thirty or more chapters. They seemed extraordinarily mindful of being inclusive, affirming the lives of Black homosexuals, transgender folks, disabled and undocumented persons, and those with police records, women, etc. Campaigns always centered around violence and systematic racism towards blacks. Racial profiling, police brutality, and racial inequality in the criminal system of the country were central to their street message.

Juveniles are defined in most states as persons up to the age of seventeen. A few states end the definition at fifteen. In September, 2000, the state of Louisiana agreed to a settlement in federal court, radically changing the way it operates juvenile prisons.[12] From 2006 until 2021, the Jackson brothers were a matter of record in Louisiana centers in Lake Charles (Calcasieu Parish), Natchitouche (Natchitouche Parish), and Monroe (Ouachita Parish). In the latter years, especially 2018 and 2019,

Dwayne and Dwight decided to be on their own, loosely tied with the BLM movement. They made their own calling cards, with a variety of lettering: WLD, WLD-JB, and WLD-OP. When their calling cards appeared on TV coverage, no one knew the actual words intended. All could be translated "bad news."

* * *

The Freddie Gray Story

A TWENTY-FIVE-YEAR-OLD BLACK MAN, Freddie Gray, was arrested by the Baltimore Police Department, April 12, 2015. Reported to be carrying an illegal knife, six officers participated in the arrest. Gray was taken to the R. Adams Crowley Trauma Center. A spinal cord injury occurred, either in the apprehension and arret or in being transported in a police van. Gray died after a week-long coma, his death ruled a homicide. The state's attorney filed numerous and varied charges.

April 21, all six officers were suspended, the circumstances of Gray's injuries unclear. Some witnesses indicated unnecessary force by the officers; denied by the department. Commissioner Anthony Batts reported that the officers did not properly secure Gray in the van. The ME agreed with the homicide charge.

The accused officers were Caesar K. Goodson, Jr., William G, Porter, Brian W. Rice, Edward M. Niero, Garett Miller, and Alicia D. White. Charges included involuntary manslaughter, second degree assault, manslaughter by vehicle, misconduct in office, and false imprisonment. The police officers were tried individually. Porter's case was ruled a mistrial, charges dropped. Officers Niero, Goodson, and Rice were acquitted ,charges dropped. Nolle prosequi was announced for the other two; all charges dropped. The federal investigation by the Department of Justice ended without any charges for the six.

In order to prevent protracted and costly litigation and apparently in an effort to heal emotions in the Baltimore community, Gray's family was awarded 6.4 million dollars.

In late April, major protests turned violent (34 arrests, 15 police officers injured). After Gray's funeral, burning and looting of businesses caused an emergency to be declared by the governor. The Maryland National Guard was deployed and curfews ordered.

* * *

The Peterson/Boseman Story

LLOYD WILLEM, SINGLE, and sixty something, the father of one child, Brandon, now eighteen already a long juvenile record at the Jefferson Parish Sheriff's office, just west of New Orleans. Recently Brandon had stolen lawn mowers, batteries from several cars and trucks, and large ceramic planters from Banting's Nursery near the river levee. He sold side-of-the street style goods like watermelon, okra, and honey farmers did.

On this late spring night, he told his dad he was meeting someone about a job and he'd be back before midnight. The someone he was meeting, Darryle, had a police record that made Brandon's rapsheet look like a school detention file. Darryle had been jailed two times before he was twenty and was currently meeting with a probation officer weekly. The job opening Darryle had offered two days earlier was as a wingman for a pizza store robbery on Clearview Parkway, a half mile from the Huey P. Long bridge. One successful heist Darryle had pulled was a Pizza Hut in Marrero on the Westbank, netting nearly three hundred dollars.

Darryle had a friend, Jackee, who rented guns, $20.00 for small pistols, if returned within 24 hours. Brandon rented one gun, a Chiappa M-22, a semi-automatic with a ten round magazine. He paid $30.00, no tax, adequate ammo thrown-in. Jackee's business was good, most of the guns obtained without paperwork. Occasionally a white kid rented from Jackee, though he assumed those sales were just for show. He charged a little extra if he could make sales to whites. A Cobra Arms Hi-Point Cq could be rented for 48 hours; same price.

Numerous businesses in the Clearview Parkway stretch of shops had contracted with a half-dozen retired cops, still wanting to keep heir heads and hands in law enforcement, earning extra cash for dinners out and entertainment. Some worked alone. Some in pairs, each with their own unmarked vehicle. They worked two, three, or four nights a week, usually 9:00 until closing, around midnight.

Owen Peterson, white, worked with Morris Boseman, black, each retired from the Kenner, Louisiana police department, and hired by the collective group at the same time. Peterson and Boseman got to be good friends, and especially were well-known by the folks at Papa John's place, two blocks from a large hospital on Clearview. The manager there prepared a pizza for each of the security guys, picked-up around eleven. They'd eat a slice or two while talking baseball, football, or Tulane and LSU sports, and take the rest home for family or neighbors. They did not wear uniforms, but they did wear shoulder holsters and packed Glock 19s, light weight and easily concealed. Owen drove a Nissan Versa and Morris a small and very rusty Tacoma.

Darryle and Brandon arrived at the Papa John's store about ten o'clock, smoked a joint or two which Darryle always had, and reviewed their plan. At eleven, the two entered the store, Darryle flashed his gu, Brandon held a cloth bag for the cash deposit. Eleven seemed a good time, hopefully catching the employees unsuspecting with no other customers in the store and no one approaching from the street. Three employees were visible, but Darryle knew there were several others in the back. He had to shout at the young man behind the cash register, effectively stopping him in his tracks, seeing the gun aimed at him or all three up front. Perhaps the youngest of the three, he raised his hands in a half-assed manner, both as if not knowing what to do and offering a hasty prayer to the man upstairs.

Peterson and Boseman, parked in a small lot, saw the young man with hands up and waving, scared and speechless. They drew their guns as Darryle started firing at the two, hoping for a quick get away. Brandon was hit twice by Peterson. Boseman went down before firing a shot.

Both Brandon and Boseman died at the scene, the pizza place splattered with blood, mostly outside the door, looking a bit like pizza sauce. Peterson tried to talk with his buddy, but there was no response. Jefferson parish police and ambulances arrived quickly. Darryle eluded the gun fire, ducked between vehicles, and escaped into the night.

Owen Peterson rode in the ambulance with a deputy to Ochsner Medical Center. A second ambulance brought Boseman to the ER. A deputy informed Morris's wife, Dorothea, of the shooting. After a full investigation of the attempted robbery, Owen was told to give his security job a rest, pending the discovery of any unwarranted gunfire at the scene.

Store employees who witnessed the incident close-up and personal cleared Peterson of any possible charges. Boseman had been felled by the would-be thief who escaped.

Owen and his wife went on an extended visit with family to Tennessee, returning in ealy summer to a new condo residence in Metairie. Death threats, both by phone and in written messages in the mail, frightened Alicia Peterson to the point of moving to another residence on the north shore of Lake Pontchartrain.

* * *

The Baba Cakes Story

JUST LIKE GARNER in New York, and Brown in Missouri, both in 2014, and Gray in Baltimore (2015) there were protests in Louisiana resultant from Brandon Willem's death in Jefferson, Louisiana. No matter what explanations were given, especially because at the time of the robbery, there may have been four guns draw, the community harangue was that Willem died unnecessarily. His uncle, Oscar, declared, " Brandon was a good boy, headed in the right direction." Truth be told, there were only three guns fired. Boseman never got a shot off. Peterson had fired five times

Protests lasted for two weeks, several of which planned to disrupt bridge traffic on the Huey P. at the busiest times of the late afternoon.

There were no protests of the death of Morris Boseman.

Peterson was through with gainful employment, but he did take a volunteer position with the Minor League baseball stadium Zephyr management, April through August, a volunteer usher.

The Minor League baseball team in Metairie, Louisiana, had gone by various names, depending on their Major League association. Once called the Zephyrs, the Baby Cakes was in deference to Baby Jesus, the small plastic baby found in every king cake in New Orleans during the carnival season.

Owen had three loves: Alicia, now married for forty-three years, law enforcement, nearly as many years, and baseball. Good friends with Lou Schwechheimer, the Baby Cakes' owner, and Arnie Beyeler, the team field manager, Owen often spent a half-hour in the Baby Cakes' dugout prior to the games. Alicia often attended the games that Owen worked, loving her seat in back of the Baby Cakes dugout.

* * *

The Muhigrdin d'Baha Story

IT'S A RARE occasion, but Black Lives Matter members or leaders are sometimes shot too. The following is taken from a winter issue of the Times Picayune, the New Orleans newspaper (Emily Lane, Jennifer Larine, and Jonathan Bullington).

New Orleans police reported that Muhigrdin d'Baha, legal last name, Maye, died at University Medical Center after taking a bullet in the thigh while riding a bicycle in Mid-City. The BLM activist from South Carolina had a brush with death ten years earlier, as reported by a girlfriend.

When in his early 20s, d'Baha was severely burned when his Charleston apartment caught fire. That near-death experience, in addition to his practice of the Baha'i faith, drove him toward the activism for which he was well-known. News of his death prompted an outpouring of mourning on social media. A vigil was held at North Charleston City Hall, just hours after the shooting. Wielding bullhorn in the wake of the shooting of Walter Scott by a white police officer, d'Baha photographs were prominent in the gathering of a small crowd in Carolina (spring, 2015).

The BLM activist grew-up in Poughkepsie, New York, but moved to South Carolina where he attended a school in Rock Hill.

D'Baha had come to New Orleans to connect with local musicians. Drums were his favorite, but he also played guitar, the flute, piano, and the marimba. He once lived in a two-room treehouse in North Carolina when the weather heated-up. He always sought the company of others in the BLM movement.

During a protest in Charleston, d'Baha drew national attention with a famed leap into a Confederate battle flag, attempting to tear it down. Since he went hurtling past yellow police tape, he was arrested for disorderly conduct.

D'Baha's shooter in New Orleans (1900 block of Bienville) was never found.

The Dominique and Iman Story

THE ATLANTA, GEORGIA metropolitan area ranks near the top among major cities of the USA with large African American populations. Georgia's racial mix is close to 70-30, white to black. More than 400,000 African Americans took residence in metropolitan Atlanta between 2012 and 2018. More recently, however, many black families have moved out of the city. Atlanta has a large LGBT contingent. Some of the suburbs (Peachtree City, Decatur) are decidedly white populations.[13]

Cole and Nigel were ten. Their twin brothers, Malik and Xavier, were almost fourteen. Dominique was the oldest boy, soon to be sixteen. They all went to the same school, all attended church with mom, and often spent time just talking at the house or at a park nearby.

D-que didn't mind C and Nigel. As long as they respected the pecking order. Basketball was the favorite pastime. D-que had college plans to play baseball if he could manage to graduate high school. The Macon community news often regaled his talent, a shortstop or maybe center fielder? His speed and potential for stealing based was noted while in Middle School.

Dominique opened a large bag of M&M peanut candies and, after taking his handful, passed them around.

"Hey, Dom, thanks for the sweet treats. Where'd ya get 'em? Walmart again?"

"Not tellin' where I shop! I keep that to myself."

"Guess nobody needs to know. I didn't mean anything, D."

Whether he meant to be or not, Dominique was the teacher and mentor for the rest. He had dropped-out of school twice since starting Ninth Grade. Mom always made sure he was re-admitted, thanks to a school board friend. Mom was determined to see D graduate. D did not share that dream. His 5th Grade Reading comprehension level had not improved since starting high school.

The folks at Hiram grocery store would not miss a few hocked pieces of fruit or a pint of cold chocolate milk. The "real cheese people" had plenty of paying customers for their America slices or chunk cheddar. These treats fit well into the baggy jeans or oversized sweats. There were usually some Ritz crackers at the house. If someone was bold enough to swipe some pre-packaged Old Farmer's ham, those zip-locked plastic bags fit well also in deep pockets.

"You back in school, right bro?"

"You know mom'll make sure of that. Yeah, for a while anyway."

"I'm thinkin' about pullin' that same stuff in a year or two," said Nigel.

"Stay in school boy! What are you? Ten? Twelve? At leastfinish Eighth Grade."

"What good is it D?" Malik asked.

No answer was offered. The candy was all gone, the bag crushed to the size of a large marble and thrown toward an overstuffed garbage can. It missed, and no one went to pick it up.

Iman joined the group, looking fresh from a shower. She was a neighbor, riding a bike that belonged to no one. All the kids had taken the bike for a spin at one time or another. No one remembered how or when the bike just showed-up one day.

D-que always came alive when Iman was around. He had never told her but he really liked her. He wished that she was seventeen, not fifteen. Iman had already taken the shape of a young lady. All the boys got their peeks and glimpses, and Iman knew it.

Laila, the boys' oldest sister, was with Iman.

"You never cleaned-up the kitchen, D! Get it done before mom gets home. You know what happened last time," Laila shouted.

"Don't worry about it, okay?" Dominique shouted back. "We got stuff to talk about. Beat!"

"I'll beat your butt, D. Then mom will get in a few good licks. Before five! You hear?"

"Yeah, yeah, yeah. Leave us guys alone."

No one said anything for a moment. When Iman looked his way, Dominique just smiled. She knew what he was smiling about.

"Later boys; stay out of trouble" the girls said together. Laila and Iman had thing to talk about too.

* * *

The Jeremiah Wilson Story

JEREMIAH WILSON WAS a small town thief who pretended to be bigger than he really was. He lived in Woodstock, Georgia, an only child with a single mother. He was friends with Dominique Richmond, by virtue of their baseball interests. Jeremiah was a pitcher, his four-seamer clocked at nearly 90 miles per hour.

The 16-year old Wilson had quite a treasure trove of stolen articles which he hoped to sell. He had athletic head and wrist bands, garden tools, packaged batteries of every size, shot glasses, ballpoint pens and other office supplies, and a dozen hunting knives. His largest hocked items were hatchets, small sledge hammers, and an array of GPS pet collars. He was a stealthy thief, amazed himself as to how easy it was to steal from certain stores.

On a recent hunt at Home Depot, combination and keyed locks were the intended prey. Most of the locks sold for less than $10.00, but it you had ten, you could net $100.00. The problem was such locks have considerable weight. When the lady at the exit door noticed his baggy sweatpants hanging low, both hands tucked into them, she stopped him to inquire. Jeremiah had a previous shoplifting incident at a Lowe's store. A security officer followed Jerimiah as he ran from the automatic door, Master locks swinging like suet feeders in twenty-five mile per hour gusts.

Ordered to stop, he decided to take his chances. The young officer would not shoot, would he?

The officer did shoot, the bullet shattering the thief's right knee. The heavy knee brace would be part of his everyday experience. Baseball would now be only as a spectator.

The officer was a new recruit, suspended until the case was resolved. Jeremiah's friend, Dominique Richmond and the neighborhood boys figured they knew how the case would end.

As Dominique walked toward Iman's house, C and Nigel kicked a beaten up, half flat soccer ball in the dusty yard. Malik and Xavier said they'd be back, a quick trip to the grocery planned. Maybe some chips or bubble gum this time?

There were no big time protests about Jeremiah's shooting. Cole, Nigel, and the other boys wondered why?

The Wilson family discovered Jeremiah's stash in several banana boxes of the infrequently used one car garage. The items would be sold at the church garage sale, held each October, hand delivered by JW. He would sit by his mother in church until he was eighteen.

* * *

The Dallas Assassinations

ALTON STERLING HAD been killed in Baton Rouge, Louisiana, Philandro Castille had been killed in Falcon Heights, Minnesota. As was the case following the shooting of other criminal suspects, there were protests against these police shootings.

In Dallas, Texas, Micah Xavier Johnson stated his intentions. He publicly stated that he wanted to kill white people, especially white police officers. Johnson ambushed and killed five police officers and injured nine others, wounding two civilians as well.

Among the police deaths were:

Senior Cpl. Lorne Ahrens, 48, a 14-year veteran of the DPD

Officer Michael Krol, 40, 9-years with the department

Sgt. Michal Smith, 55, a former Army Ranger, had been with the department for 27 years

Officer Brent Thompson, 43, a former Marine, seven years with the DPD

Each of these officers have their stories; family and friends who mourn their loss. There were no street protests for the officers, no buildings burned, no businesses destroyed.[14]

*　*　*

The Sandra Brown Story

IT'S NOT UNUSUAL to see a police officer at a large grocery, big box store, shopping center. Officers commonly serve the public at banks, bars, and clubs, and at church or community fairs. Presumably their presence is to prevent shoplifting and other thefts, to settle disputes, etc.

People who watch a lot of television, and don't block-out commercial messages, are likely familiar with the "security monitor during a bank robbery" scenario. Bank guests hit the floor as the robbers' shouted commands, announcing a holdup. One of the patrons, on the floor and expecting trouble while next to a uniformed security monitor says, "Aren't you going to do something?"

The uniformed man says, "Oh, no. I'm not a security officer. I'm a monitor. I just tell you if there's a robbery. Then he says, "There's a robbery."

The dental monitor commercial is similar. With every possible cotton swab and dental apparatus of numerous sorts in his mouth, the dental monitor offers, "This is one of the worst cavities I've ever seen." As he starts to leave for lunch, the man in the chair questions in his best "mouth-full-of-stuff" desperation, "Aren't you going to fix it?" The reply is not helpful: "I'm not the dentist. I'm the dental monitor."

In our country, especially in the last twenty years, dentists were not being attacked and/or killed by dentist haters. But plenty of police personnel were being shot, some killed, some injured, just because of their profession.

Sandra Brown was proud to be the first police woman her family and friends had seen. Her uncle and her oldest brother had served in various law enforcement roles for years in Mississippi. Parents no longer living, her father passed away when Sandra was thirty-one, her mother succumbing to pancreatic cancer two years later. Sandra had just completed police training in Mobile.

Uncle Larry and bother Rudy had not encountered life threatening situations throughout their many years. And that was okay with them. Sandra sought excitement and even danger, the TV and movie type.

A private event, hosted by local politicians needing positive publicity was scheduled for the weekend, honoring the medical professionals of Mobile and Biloxi. Most of the crowd would be pediatricians. Sandra's husband, Derek, was to give the keynote address to kick-off the celebration. He had been a prominent doctor at Children's Hospital in New Orleans, but now was in private practice.

Uncle Larry and Rudy were part of a six-man crew to handle parking, traffic, and general surveillance for the event, 6:00-11:00 PM. Following a catered dinner, about 7:30, Sgt. Larry Brown saw the attack coming. Two gunmen in dark sweats and stocking hats stood only a few car lengths from udy, directing traffic at the busy street next to the hotel. Point blank pistol shots rang-out and reverberated among the tall buildings of Water Street. Brother Rudy was down. The sergeant's return fire appeared to hit one of the two perps, racing on foot from the scene, away from the bay. Derek was into his thirty-minute address to theseveral hundred gathered. He noted Sandra's departure from the speaker's table. In attractive dinner attire, she saw Uncle Larry's tearful and telling eyes that Rudy was the victim of an attack outside.

The police department brass at the ER were hopeful as Sandra approached from a police cruiser. EMTs had brought Rudy back to life, doctors working feverously to save him. Derek and many friends joined Sandra at the hospital for the remainder of the stressful night.

Rudy survived but was severely handicapped in speech and mobility. He was offered employment at the department, but he chose to end his career and assist at police academies held in Mississippi.

Local reporting of the shooting described the incident as random, no apparent motive. Neither of the attackers was found. Uncle Larry had serious discussions with Sandra about continuing in the profession, all to no avail.

***

The Calvin Dunne Story

CALVIN DUNNE AND his wife, Nancy, met at a shopping mall food court in Charlotte, North Carolina. He always called her Nance, her family insisted in her full name, adding her middle name, Marie. She liked the short form. Married for two years now, no children, though not for the lack of trying.

Calvin's vacation was coming-up in a week. They'd go to Turks and Caicos Islands in the Caribbean. He had just one week so she, an RN at Novant health-Presbyterian Medical Center in Charlotte was ready for a break too. Nance worked in ICU, mostly with new borns, not yet ready to go home with mom and dad. If she could relax and enjoy the islands with Calvin, perhaps they could conceive and look toward a healthy baby?

Calvin joined the Charlotte-Mecklenburg Police Department two years before their marriage. His job was stressful at times, but much less than hers. Nance always had a hard time in the mornings as Calvin left for his shift, 8:00 AM to 6:00PM, four days a week. The department had 1200 officers and a support staff of 300 but Calvin occasionally worked on Saturday or Sunday or both, four or five hours as needed.

Chic-Fil-A was their favorite lunch spot. The Chic-Fil-A Deluxe and Grilled Chicken Club sandwiches, waffle fries, and a soft drink always arrived quickly, service they appreciated. They talked about the anticipated time off. Friends who had been to Turks and Caicos wished that they could go along.

Calvin's parents had gifted the couple with the week stay at Beaches Resort, a Christmas present. The elder Dunnes would have their first grandchild, and already had a list of names for consideration, both boy and girl.

"Your dad said he checked on the reservations. Did he tell you?"

"Only three times since Sunday. You ready to go?"

"Been packed for a week. Can't wait!"

"The long range weather forecast looks good in the islands. Low 70s and 80s. I guess we can live with that?"

"Should we plan our days? Maybe make some arrangements for special happenings?"

"Let's just play it by ear, day-to-day. No bed time or get up time. Just relax and enjoy the time together."

She smiled at him and squeezed his hand, sipping a Diet Coke, knowing how he had intended their time together. That was her plan too.

Calvin had a two-day seminar at the department just prior to the vacation. Police departments throughout the country had scheduled training sessions on "improvised weaponry" used by radicalized individuals and terror groups since many attacks had occurred in the world and in the United States in recent years.

Such attacks on the public were more common than anyone wanted to see. In March of 2016, an SUV attack at the University of North Carolina at Chapel Hill had gotten everyone's attention on the east coast. Most people considered such attacks a jihadis terrorism.[15]

In 2010, CNN ran a story calling for deploying pickup trucks as "moving machings" to mow down enemies of Allah. In 2014 Isis called for lone wolf attacks using vehicles as weapons. In October of that year an attack occurred at a light rail station in Jerusalem. There was the Paris attack in November of 2015, warranting French air attacks on Isis in

Syria and Iraq. By August, six suspects had been taken into custody with charges of criminal terrorist conspiracy, three more charged as accomplices in December.

The July 14, 2016 attack in Nice, France, was perhaps the most destructive. A 19-ton cargo truck drove into crowds celebrating Bastille Day on the Promenade des Anglais. Eighty-six people died and nearly five hundred others were injured. A Tunisian resident of France, Mohammed Bouhiel, was shot and killed by police to end the carnage.[16]

A Christmas market in Berlin, 2016, was the site of a tractor-trailer incident, killing twelve. In March of 2017, an SUV drove into a crowded sidewalk at the Westminster Bridge in London; four fatalities.

Police departments in the USA believed that this terrorist tactic would be copied by others, perhaps just to kill law enforcement officers. Prevention was the hoped for focus of the seminars, as well as police action to apprehend the offenders following such copycat attacks.

Returning home earlier tha expected on Friday afternoon, in uniform and still technically on duty, Officer Dunne noticed an apparent elderly black lady driving eratically thirty yerds in front of him. When she pulled to a sudden stop at a caution light, Eastway Drive and Goodwin Avenue, he got out and quietly tapped on her window. He thought she either had a very bad hair day or wore a really cheap wig. She seemed to be talking to herself or maybe singing along with a very loud radio.

The window rolled down and a small handgun was aimed directly at his chest. She said nothing as three shots rang out, no other vehicles at the intersection. Dunne fell to the street as the Chevy Camaro sped away.

The autopsy done late on Friday night determined that any of the three 9mm bullets from the M&P Shield would have ended the officer's life.

The Rooney Porter Story

"Where did he ever get that name?" Walter asked his wife. "His given name was Karl." Walter and Millie Cummins sat in weathered wooden rocking chairs for most of the late afternoon at the Matthew's Funeral Home in Orange, Texas. They lived two doors down from Rooney.

"Never was told" Millie quietly offered. "Your father, rest his soul, once said an army buddy gave it to him."

"He always talked religion in conversations with friends," Walter remembered. "I don't think he ever missed church."

Another half hour passed without much talk as family and friends walked by, saying "Howdy folks" before waiting in the long line of mourners. The East Texas community of Beaumont and Rose City was saddened three days earlier as Rooney Porter was killed by a sniper's bullet, exiting from his patrol car after stopping a speedster on I-10 West. One shot was all it took to end the life of a twelve-year veteran on the police force.

Rooney's wife, Sarah, had sat with their three children, aged ten, eight, and six, on Sunday evening at the wake, 6:00 to 9:00. Hundreds who knew Rooney expressed their sorrow and sympathy with lots of tears and many police stories that Rooney had told.

Sheriff Teo Ortiz stopped to speak with Walter.

"Just can't understand it, Walt, the blatant disregard for life by some people. I'm so sorry for the passing of your son-in-law. He was one of our best, loved by everyone on the force and by everyone in town. He did so much for the youth here."

Walter and Millie did not respond. Words were too hard and difficult. Tears never seemed to dry as they huddled in a sometimes stiff northerly breeze. They nodded kindly. Sheriff Ortiz understood. His wife had recently been laid to rest after suffering with heart problems for three years. Ortiz had announced his retirement at the end of the year.

Rev. Ron Beasely, pastor at New Life Baptist, met Sheriff Ortiz as he came to the door.

"Anything new on the case, Teo?"

"Nothing today or yesterday. The trail is already cold. Just a young guy that rumbled out of town toward Vidor. Hooded sweat, blue jeans, boots, on a hog larger than any we have on the force. Three witnesses could not be sure if the biker was the culprit. Deer rifle, the weapon."

"I'm going in to help with the kids Walter. We'll take them to our house 'till Sarah gets home. Tomorrow will be another tough and tiring day."

"I'll wait here. Better than being inside with all that crying and tears. Not sure I have any tears left, his red, white, and blue handkerchief sadly needing a replacement.

Police Chief John Mina, an army vet, announced his retirement from the department. There were rumors that he might consider candidacy for Orange County Sheriff.

***

The Ronnie Wilcox Story

"When will daddy be home, mommy?"

Helen Wilcox got this question often. Debra, her five-year-old asked most of the time. Big brother, Jeff, soon to be eight, had gotten out of the habit, but he was wary too.

"About another hour, honey. Daddy said he'd take you guys to Baskin-Robins, right?"

"Right!" Deb said. "You going with us this time?"

"Not tonight sweetheart. Maybe Daddy will bring my favorite home? Will you remind him?"

In unison, "Daddy forgets, but we'll tell him. Chocolate mint again?"

"Chocolate mint," Helen Cox said with a big smile.

Lots of promises were made to the kids. And many promises to her. Ronnie kept most of them.

The usual "Be careful, okay?" was said each time Ron left for his shift at the Slidell Police Department.

Each time, the promise was the same, "I'll see you tonight. You know I'll be careful."

The department was on Brown Switch Road. Slidell was a growing city, ten minutes from New Orleans. Ron's promotion allowed him a schedule which they both liked, most weekends free for family fun.

Like many policemen, Ronnie loved his job. Helen and the kids were very proud of him. The whole department had just honored him and four others with a small celebration at a Parish on Military Road. Helen was invited to provide the fanfare, which she handled expertly.

An hour later, Debra asked again. Ronnie was working a 7:00 A to 5:00P.

"Maybe daddy stopped for some dry cleaning, honey. Go tell Jeffie to get ready. I can taste the chocolate mint already."

Sometimes the ice cream treat had to wait. Another late dinner for two wasn't unusual.

The phone rang. The number was a familiar one, from the department. "Helen …Captain McHardy here. Helen" …and the long pause was telling.

An elderly sitter next door came quickly after Helen's urgent call. Katherine Jones was always on duty for Ronnie, the policeman.

A patrol car picked-up Helen. The ten-minute drive to the ER at Doctor's Hospital seemed like ten hours.

Ronnie was unconscious with very slight movement of the eyes and lips. Helen was allowed to go in, the surgical team stepping aside, with little hope of any sustained life. With her tears streaming, it seemed to her that he needed to say something.

AS best he could, Ronnie Wilcox managed, "Tell the kids …" or "Take the kids …" and then he was gone. Helen knew both of the intended messages, one about ice cream, the other that he loved them.

The Ryan Winston Story

NELLIE CONFORTO WAS no stranger to firearms. She had her own handgun, a Smith & Wesson Bodyguard 380, a gift from her father on her nineteenth birthday as she finished her first year of college, pre-law, and looked forward to completing the program in record time. Nellie worked hard at every new venture, including work at a firing range in Tuscaloosa where her fiancé had proposed to her just a week ago.

"You did talk with my father, right Ryan? It's what he would expect?"

"Of course I did, Nel. We had a great conversation about you. About us."

Nellie wanted the whole story.

"Well, first he told me he'd shoot me with my own gun if I didn't treat you right. He knew that the two of us would be good for each other, though both still wet behind the ears."

Mr. Conforto was often with Nellie at the firing range or at a gun show. He wanted the two to wait another year or so, you doing well in school and me in my first year with the police department.

Ryan and Nellie were not in a hurry to have children, both having great plans for separate careers.

Mr. Conforto had four guns at the house; one pistol and three rifles, mostly for deer hunting. Nllie was a marksman, rivaling anything that Sean Hannity bragged about on talk radio. He was a retired policeman, enjoying his various hobbies, hunting deer in Mississippi, and traveling the country.

Happy as a lark, Nellie went to class every day, her future bright and exciting. Then one day, her father texted her to come home immediately. Ryan was at the ER at Northport Medical Center. He and others at a four-man backup unit at the Wingate Apartments had been ambushed. There were many injuries. The apartment complex had a history.

Thanks to a friend who knew the quickest route to Northport, Nellie expected the worst. There was no stopping her, She dragged her dad into the building, demanding to see Ryan. The doctor at the door of the surgery unit shook his head to try to warn them. Two gun shots to the chest had ended the life of a young policeman minutes earlier.

It was the third shooting and death of a policeman for the city of Tuscaloosa, and spring had not officially sprung. Nellie and her dad were allowed to spend a few moments with Ryan. Ryan's family from North Carolina would not arrive until the weekend.

Some police shootings end the life of career lawmen. This one ended the life of a fellow just beginning to serve and protect. The shooter was apprehended, holed-up at an abandoned garage near the apartment buildings. Refusing the warnings of the Swat team, and charging with gun blazing, his life ended quickly too.

Nellie had met Ryan's parents only one time, on a Christmas visit to Charlotte, She offered her engagement ring to Ryan's mom, but his mom insisted that Nellie keep it. She would treasure Ryan's memory as much as his parents would. Both promisedto keep in touch. Plans were made for a graduation from law school get-together in the Roll Tide city.

* * *

The Harold Martin Story

"Nothing But Peace and Quiet" was part of the claim for Brady, Texas, a town of about 5,000, with not a lot of color: 58 percent white, 38 percent Latino, and just 2 percent black. It didn't boast many millionaires, the median household income in the low $20,000.00 category.

Most residents in Brady, while maybe not buying into total peace and quiet, certainly did not consider their community one of danger, violence, or rowdy behavior. It's location at 31 degrees latitude and 99 degrees longitude makes it the closest town to the geographic center of Texas, the second largest state in the union. (There's one or two trivia questions with that info).

The wildflowers of Texas in the spring, especially in the hill country, are the attraction that brings hoards of visitors to the state. Brady is one of the best places to see the bluebonnets, black-eyed Susans, Mexican hats, Indian blankets, paintbrushes, and phlox. Brady often makes the #1 spot on the list of nice (some would say-sleepy) small towns in the Lone Star state.

On this late January day, the calm and quiet was broken by gun fire, and the killing of a veteran police officer, Harold Martin. A long time Texan, Harold was born in the Rio Grande Valley, his early years took him to Austin because his father's political career, and then to San Antonio. With four other friends, he was part-owner of a Riverwalk café. Before turning forty, he and his wife, Clara, moved to Brady. He began a career in law enforcement as one of ten sworn officers on the town's police force. An auxiliary staff of nine made for a smooth, comfortable operation, the police maintaining a presence on the streets with tourists and among the permanent residents. Officer Martin knew just about everyone who called Brady home. He and Clara had no children.

Central Texas can get a little wintery in January-February, temperatures ranging from 40 to 60 degrees. The annual high temp is close to 80 with an average low of 51 degrees.

On January 29, Officer Martin made plans with Clara for a twentieth wedding anniversary lunch at a local diner. Harold's parents lived in Arizona, retired and loving it. Clara's parents were no longer living, each a lung cancer casualty. Harold's dad promised a big dinner in New Braunfels.

Clara Martin worked for a national investment company in San Antonio for twelve years and then as a nurse in Brady. She anticipated retiring in the not-to-distant future. Harold promised the same. Though leaving the police would not be easy. Their plans were to retire before the age of sixty in the Fredericksburg area, where Clara had a sister.

Martin was off-duty at noon for the anniversary date, the Deer Lake Diner, a favorite eatery. He parked his vehicle at the small and packed lot, a lake bordering the property. Two shots from a lone gunman put the officer down among numerous others arriving for dinner. Martins' life ended instantly.

Harold's best buddy, a fellow officer, intercepted Clara upon arrival. Three other patrol cars were at the scene, light flashing with a small crowd gathered behind the police tape. Clara was taken to Heart of Texas Hospital in Brady where she was allowed a brief time with her fallen husband.

Three witnesses who saw and heard the attack shared similar information with the investigating officers. The shooter appeared to be a young Black man, perhaps six feet tall and one hundred fifty pounds, dirty Champion sweats, bottom to top, gray. A mailman, being less than thirty feet from the gunfire, and two women, reported seeing a Toyota, rusty red, leaving the parking lot. There was apparently no conversation between the shooter and Martin, the incident lasting less than a minute.

Texas wildflowers had two months or more before popping-up and coloring the countryside. The townspeople talked about the shooting for months, nothing like it having happened in decades. Clara contacted the Brady police regularly from her sister's house, all without closure to her policeman, who loved the peace and quiet of Brady.

* * *

The Leon Starks Story

Julian Ford and Leon Starks were not rookie cops, but they were the least experienced on the Pigeon Forge police force. Each usually worked with a more seasoned officer, but, when they were a team, they shared a Crown Victoria or other souped-up ride. There was always an argument about who would drive.

A salt-and-pepper duo, Ford was white; Starks black. Starks had been named for the heavy weight boxer, Leon Spinks, who had defeated Mohammed Ali in a split decision heavy weight bout. Julien's given name was in respect for his uncle, a careen policeman with the department in Nashville, Tennessee.

Ford had recently proposed to Sandra Kelly, a college girlfriend and a pediatric nurse at Urgent Care of the Smokies. The wedding was being planned for the holiday season.

In two weeks the nation and the Dollywood family-fun community would celebrate Thanksgiving. Starks and his wife of four years had two children; two-year-old Delaney, and an infant, Laramie. The Fords and Starks families often had dinner together, sometimes the children joining the party at the Ford's house or a local fastfood place.

Dollywood, like the other major fun parks in the country, had well-trained security, with little or no reported civil disturbances ever. Crowd control was largely the job of the park staff, always expert at the task. The summer and the holiday seasons were the busiest times at the park. Ford and Starks often contracted to support the Dollywood staff, sometimes in uniform and other times undercover. Subdued police presence was the rule, young officers favored over older or retired personnel.

Henry Frank, well-known by law enforcement in Sevier County, was the oldest of two children of the Frank family, his criminal record as long as a late summer day in the Volunteer state.

At the age of eighteen, the locals just called him Hank Frank. The department had numerous names for him, one more demeaning than the other. Henry Frank was as disgusting, careless youth, with no regard for friend or foe.

Hank's sister Wanda, learned the criminal trade from big brother, often hearing wild stories about Hank. Frank Sr., who had spent more years in prison than he had with the kids, was no gentleman. The wife had run-off with another man at the age of twenty-six. Many of the unsavory males in Pigeon Forge referred to Wanda as Wanna, a question, or, more exactly, an offer, she heard many late nights in the bars and honkytonks around town. Her usual reply was, "Why not cowboy? What do I have to lose?" Neither brother nor sister, thank God, had any children.

Arrested twice by Ford and Starks, Hanks' hatred for the pair was public knowledge. One arrest for petty larceny, the other for attempted armed robbery of a Quick Stop store and gas station. Somehow Hanks was released and on the street again. Hank's animosity for police in general dominated his sorry life.

Hank Jr. lived mostly off his few friends, two of whom always seemed to have resources. Getting a gun, borrowed, of course, was as easy in Tennessee as it was in any city in the USA. Come hell or high water, he focused on and often shadowed Ford and Starks. Soon one or both would pay!

Three days after Thanksgiving, Julian was given strict orders to take a few days off to help with preparations for the wedding. It would not be a large ceremony, but his list of "To Dos" from his father, her mother, and her, looked challenging for his two-day break from policing. "Yes mom, yes mom-to-be, and yes ma'am" were his respectful replies. This Monday and Tuesday would be busy but maybe fun.

Leon worked a three-hour shift just inside the admissions gate at Dollywood. His police cruiser was parked outside the park entrance, so he often went in and out to check with the department of with Julian. Leon always felt safe when in his patrol car.

Henry Frank had never been to Dollywood, and never would. He waited near the Starks vehicle, knowing the cop would eventually show. Just after nine o'clock, Starks walked to the car, sat inside, the door still open. A quick firing of the 38-special, all three shots hitting the upper body, and the life of a promising your policeman and family man ended in minutes.

In the far parking lot, a friend's car quickly left the Dollywood perimeter. The car was later discovered at a local bar and grill, thanks to a security camera recording all entrances at the park. Just before Christmas, Henry Frank was arrested for the assignation of Office Leon Starks. The pistol, with fingerprints, was found in a trash can far from the main gate. Frank had the promise of life imprisonment or maybe worse. Convicted of the shooting, his sentencing was scheduled for February 19, his twenty-fourth birthday.

The Gerald Holland Story

It was icy in New Orleans in January, 2017. Carole and Gerald Holland had just dropped-off Suze and Danny at school, Suze in Kindergarten and big brother in Second Grade. It was cold and unusually breezy in Harvey, ten minutes from the Louisiana Superdome. A light dusting of wintery mix had fallen overnight. Parents and kids were dressed in whatever winter clothes they could find. Sgt. G. Holland was in his uniform and a warm police department jacket, though he looked the least dressed for the day of the four. Sometimes the school kids in the area bundled with winter clothes even when the temperature dropped to the low 50s.

Gerald Holland would begin his patrol duty at 9:00 AM and work through the day, going home sometime after seven in the evening. Sgt. Holland never saw his next shift, his wife, or his kids again.

At he intersection of Manhattan Blvd. and Lapalco Blvd. in Harvey, a black Ford G-150 pulled alongside, a lone driver huddled at the wheel, with the passenger side window rolled mostly down. Holland's side mirror had a light coating of ice or frost which blurred any view of traffic behind or on his left. He rolled his window down, hoping to scrape the ice or some of it off the mirror. Cold fingernails sometimes worked.

Blood and flesh blasted Carole in the face and upper body when three shots rang out killing Sgt. Holland instantly, his vehicle easing into the intersection where it was sideswiped by a small compact, both cars now with steam and radiator fluids blowing upward toward the traffic lights.

Carole, in shock, was taken from the car by firemen and police. Ochsner Hospital was less than a mile from the intersection. Her husband arrived almost one hour later DOA.

A YOUfit store manager in a light pickup behind the F-150 got the license plate number as the truck sped away, going north on Manhattan. The store manager stopped to check on the occupants of the vehicles and stayed to provide whatever information he could remember. His pickup also had ice on the windshield, wipers, and hood. So, other than the license plate, little was noted about Ford truck. He simply described the truck as black, large, knobby tires, with no memorable markings on the bumper or back windshield.

The truck was discovered at the Waffle House lot shortly after noon, in front of a large glass office building. It had been stolen that morning on Vulcan Street in Harvey, the owner not home, reported to be on a hunting lease in Mississippi.

* * *

The Luis Brocamontes Story

CAROLE HOLLAND AND two young children had lost their husband and father to an assassin's gunfire. She had not been hit by the barrage of bullets, but was not released by the ER until she felt ready to go and the police had asked all of their questions.

Carole told the investigating officers that she knew of no problems for Gerald on the force or among the family and friends. Local media reported that Gerald was killed. Carole's word for the attack was assassination. Th wife of a policeman knew of the many assaults on law enforcement, both locally and nationally.

At a new conference held in the evening of the assault, Carole said that she and Gerald had spent some time in the early morning with a local TVs news show. The main subject of the show concerned the October shooting of two police officers in Sacramento, California, 2014. That attack, also a "just because they were policemen" episode, was at a Motel ^ six-hour rampage by an illegal immigrant, Luis Brocamontes. Brocamontes had been previously deported to Mexico twice. The news report centered on the June 14, 2017, court hearing, where Brocamontes went postal, smiling at the judge and a half-dozen police officers, commenting, "I wish I had killed more of the ……. cops." He said, "I regret that I only killed two of them!"

Questioned by the judge if Brocamontes had any regrets at all, he said, "I don't regret anything at all." Deputy Danny Oliver and Michael Davis, Jr. were the two killed. A co-defendant in the attack was Janelle Monroy, she burst into tears because of those "cold" statements, causing her to be removed from the courtroom.

Many months passed as Brocamontes was held in custody. After admitting again his dastardly deed, his lawyers fought for life imprisonment rather than the death penalty. The legal maneuvers were completed by January 15, 2918, and the trial began.

As of July, 2024, Brocamontes is being held in San Quinton, awaiting his death.

Strange, isn't it, how a life can be snuffed-out in an instant, and another life can take ten years or more, after the sentence is pronounced![17]

* * *

The Rodney Abrams Story

THE HENDERSON FUNERAL Home, Forest Orchard, Oklahoma, fall, 2017. A long line of mourners awaited the viewing and wake o Officer Rodney Abrams, 29, a local policeman. Officer Abrams was ambushed in an assassin's attack when responding to a 911 call. The Hard-to-hear plea of the phone call reported that a physical assault on a young woman, the perp apparently having two small handguns with the threat to use them both.

Abrams had arrived at the address alone, backup promised to arrive only minutes away. But backup was delayed by a hit-and-run at an intersection in the town of only five thousand people. Abrams took two shots to the upper body as he cautiously approached the entrance of a modest home.

Abrams had drawn his lightweight Austrian Glock 19, expecting a fire fight. Neighbors reported two gun shots in separate calls to local police.

RAMA

Several who lived on South Oak Drive later reported hearing and seeing a yellow van, A/C and Heating printed on the side.

A month prior, Abrams and a partner, Hollis Furness, had made a drug bust in the same neighborhood, with assistance from two other police units. A methamphetamine operation our of a two-car garage had lead the radio and television news for a week. The officers were praised for their efforts in shutting down the drug operation, which finally involved nine arrests from three small towns.

The description of the shooter was not great: average height and weight, dark brown hair, dark pants and hooded top pullover, black tennies, maybe Converse high tops. The van had Texas plates but the numbers were disputed among the three most reliable witnesses. They did agree that several threes were part of the dirty plate.

Officer Abrams had weak vitals when EMTs took him from the scene. The Oklahoma Surgical Hospital was to be the delivery. But the loss of a lot of blood caused them to go to the St. John Urgent Care Center, the closest facility to Forest Orchard. The diagnosis was DOA, all fifteen rounds still in the officer's pistol.

Amy Abrams was advised of the shooting as well as Rodney's parents who lived in Tulsa. Not even the EMT personnel were able to communicate with the fallen policeman. The Abrams family was expecting their first child with the delivery of a healthy baby boy. Camile and George Abrams had hoped many more children for their son.

Forest Orchard had chiefly whitecollar employment, many more households without children than with youngsters, the average household income about $75,000.00 a year. With the birth of Rodney Jr., there was one more child in town, but a kid without a father.

The yellow van was discovered in a DOT tractor shed at the Tulsa State Fairgrounds off I-64 near Jefferson Terrace after a police chase ended in the area. That chase ended without apprehension on the two youths on cycles. Witnesses of the Abrams attack positively identified the van, Texas license plate #33834, reported stolen in Denton, Texas, near Dallas, two days before the shooting in Forest Orchard.

The Riley Williams Story

RILEY WILLIAMS RETIRED from the St. Charles Parish Sheriff's Department after twenty-four years of exemplary service. He was a veteran of the Iraq war, serving with distinction in Operation Desert Storm, January, 1919.

Riley needed to be out-and-about. Though his wife, Candice, pushed him toward various hobbies, none struck his fancy, and he was not a reader, handyman, or small engine repairman.

Offered a part-time job at an Ochsner Hospital Emergency Room in Gretna, Louisiana, he signed-on for the morning and early afternoon stint, three days a week. On most days, Riley stopped at a Brothers Gas Station and convenience store on Lapalco Blvd. to talk with the several middle eastern employees, sharing with them his experience in Iraq.

The Williams lived in Kenner, a growing city in Jefferson Parish, just before St. Charles Parish and near Lake Pontchartrain.

The Williams children, all boys, lived and worked in Houston; two married, the third still single.

By 11:00 o'clock AM, the injured from the night before or early morning had been registered and processed, were receiving treatment and/or diagnosis, and some had already been released. Many days the traffic in-and-out was similar, elderly with shortness of breath, kidney, heart, or stomach concerns, and occasional vehicular or workplace injuries.

Riley struck-up conversations with anyone who wanted to talk. He believed some light conversation while patients who waited to see a doctor was part of the ER's service. He had lots of stories to share, both police stories and those from the war.

For a change of pace and some fresh air, Riley often spent time on a leisurely walk outside, especially around lunchtime. He bought healthy snacks to work, always packed for him by a health-conscious wife. When they went out to eat, Candice preferred the early specials at Picadilly

Cafeteria The Outback Steakhouse as Riley's preference: coconut shrimp, baked potato, and a house salad.

Riley carried a weapon when on duty, in his case a rarely used .45 caliber pistol. He knew how to handle many guns, always ready, if needed. In a light drizzle on this walk, Riley put on a Saints windbreaker, oversized, which, though not intended, disguised him as a policeman on security detail. He stopped at a metal bench to tie a shoe. Two pistol shots at close range parted the muggy air. Riley never saw the attack coming. Another law enforcement officer had been killed in nearby Harahan, Louisiana, just because he was police. Just because he wore the blue.

Candice sold the house, moved to Houston, and tried her best to get the # 3 hitched. She wanted and very much needed grandkids, now nearing sixty. One of the boys, often with a spouse, invited her to dinner, sometimes in and other times out. When out, it was almost always the cafeteria for early bird specials.

NOTE: The next three stories are quite brief. I'll make them a reader's quiz. Are they real stories or fictional? How do you know one way or another? Does it really matter which?

* * *

The Justin Billa Story

ONE MIGHT WONDER what the life of a police officer is like every day? How many times does he or she get called to check-out civil or domestic violence, burglary, gun shots fired, or suspected drug offenses? How often are police officers called to vehicular accidents? How many traffic citations do police officers write per month? How often does an officer fire his gun a month or a year?

Officer Justin Billa had been declared Mobile Officer of the Month, June 16, 2016, Toulminville, Alabama. He had made two felony arrests, seventeen misdemeanor arrests, was called for back[uphelp eleven times, and had written two dozen traffic tickets; one hundred and thirty-five service calls in the month of May his total.

Toulminville was a small settlement on the property of Harry Theophilus Toulmin, Sherriff of Mobile County in the 1880s. Serious crime was the case in the 1980s and 1990s, once an upper-middle class suburb of Mobile.

Called to a homicide investigation in early 2917, officer Billa was killed by Robert Hollie, who had barricaded himself in a house, after killing his wife, a two-hour standoff following. Billa also had a one-year old son.

* * *

The Chase Maddox Story

CHASE MADDOX, FIVE years with the police department of Locust Grove, Georgia, a town in north-central Henry County, population six thousand. Trying to serve a warrant, Maddox was killed by a single pistol shot. Two other deputies were also shot but not seriously hurt after the suspect refused to cooperate.

Maddox was twenty-six, his wife, Alex, gave birth to their second child a week later. That child, Bodie Allen, was named after a grandfather, a veteran of Henry County Police Department. Hundreds attended the funeral of Chase Maddox at Glen Haven Baptist Church in McDonough.

The Paul Bauer Story

CHICAGO AREA POLICE officers attended the funeral of Police Commander Paul Bauer, age 59, thirty-one years with the department. A model police officer, Bauer was shot multiple times, the suspect arrested and his weapon recovered. Bauer had a wife and an early teenage daughter. The Nativity of Our Lord Catholic church was SRO for the Saturday funeral.

* * *

The Markeith Lloyd Story

POLICE OFFICERS DON'T spend all of their time at the police station. They live in the community. They go to the barber shop, the bank, movie theaters, and shopping malls. Officers go to restaurants and grocery stores. They attend their children's baseball, basketball, and soccer games. Sometimes they are in full uniform. Sometimes they dress like you do. Police officers are people like you.

January 9, 2018, Orange County, Orlando, Florida. More than a dozen schools are on lockdown, traffic is snarled for hours, and not because Disney World is extra busy. There has been gun fire, and at least one policeman has been killed.

Markeith Lloyd had been wanted for murder for more than six months, The black man had been in prison for ten years but was out on probation now for half as long. His criminal record was long, including drug charges. He killed his pregnant girlfriend, December 13, 2017.

Lloyd brashly proclaimed one of his goals on Facebook. He wanted to be named one of America's most wanted!

One late spring morning, Lloyd was spotted at a Walmart store and reported to Master Sargeant Debra Clayton, who was at the store at the time. In Clayton's chase, she was shot, pronounced dead at the Orlando Regional Medical Center, CPR attempts having failed.

Other police officers joined in the chase and apprehension of Lloyd, who had carjacked a vehicle and drove to an apartment complex. In his escape, other shots were fired, one or more hitting a police car but not injuring the driver. A crash of two motorcycles, however, resulted in the death of a second officer, Norman Lewis.

Sgt. Debra Clayton was married and had one son. She was one of the first responders in the Pulse Club tragedy in June a year earlier where forty-nine were killed and many others injured. Debra Clayton and Norman Lewis were black police officers.[18]

* * *

When will it all stop? An opinion

IT? THE SHOOTING (and, in many cases, the killing of people by police officers).

Answer: It won't!

The shooting, maiming and/or killing of people by police will not stop until those who are committing crimes, especially acts of violence against others, start obeying the commands of law enforcement. Cease and desist works. Stop or I'll shoot still should work. At the very least, you won't end-up on a stretcher headed to the morgue or a hospital in critical condition.

I saw two videos this morning. One was the shooting of a teen in Columbus, Ohio: My'Khia Bryant. This 16-year-old girl was yielding a knife, attacking one or more other girls. One of the other girls or a friend or on-looker called 911, to indicate that the knife attack was happening. An officer responded, shot the attacker, apparently firing four shots, killing the teenager.[19]

Protests (and, hopefully, only peaceful protests) in Columbus, Ohio, and likely, in other cities and communities of our country, will occupy "news" broadcasts for weeks, especially in the podcast form.

An NBA "star" tweeted a brief comment about the incident, using the officer's phote, saying, "You're next!" How untimely! How ignorant! How unAmerican! With pressure from someone or somewhere, the round ball idiot deleted his tweet.[20]

The second video was from a pregame situation in Wrigley Field, before a Cubs' game. Two black youths brought an American flag into short centerfield. They also brought lighter fluid and matches. Rick Monday, longtime Dodger first baseman, saw what was happening, ran toward the flag on the ground, grabbed it, and rescued it from an intended flag burning. The third base coach for the Dodgers ran to the scene and, ostensibly, would have done what Monday did. Others (Steve Garvey) supported Mondy's action. [21]

Are YOU feeling a little better about these everyday American stories, real or fictitious?

***

Police Shootings Statistics

LATE IN 2018, forty-six police officers in our country had been shot and killed while serving the citizens of their communities. Stats were similar for 2017.

In DeKalb County, Georgia, a police officer was shot after a routine traffic stop at Chandler and Tilson roads near I-20. The suspect ran from his car in a Piggly Wiggly parking lot with the officer in pursuit on foot. The suspect pulled a gun, shot the officer, and was eventually found by a large scramble of police cars. A police dog was shot by the suspect, hiding at a business nearby. Two days later the canine was in critical condition at a local veterinarian office. Police shot and killed the run-away suspect.

In Georgia alone, there had been eighty-nine shootings of police officers during the year.

I thought an update on police shootings might be helpful for my readers. The following are figures for the years 2020, 2021, 2022, and 2023:

2020 police shootings of white men: 500-plus
Police shootings of black men: 250

2021 police shootings of white men: 490
Police shootings of black men: 230

2022 police shootings of white men: 340
Police shootings of black men: 210

2023 police shootings of white men: 320
Police shootings of black men: 220

The stats for fatal shootings differ, the blacks being much higher; no explanation given.

Incarcerations for white and black men stats are for the year 2021 per 100,000:

Black incarcerations: 528
White incarcerations: 157
Hispanic incarcerations: 145

Again, readers may have their own answers as to why the disparity.

Random Thoughts on Hatred in American Culture/Summer, 2024

1. I'm Christian! I'm conservative! I (We) conservatives must intimidate our liberal counterparts? Perhaps Shaw had a different thought in mind, but he makes a lot of sense: "Hatred is the coward's revenge for being intimidated." (George Bernard Shaw)[22]

2. "Hatred is something peculiar. You will always find it strongest and most violent where there is the lowest degree of culture." (von Goethe) What am I to conclude about the actions, beliefs, and behaviors of my liberal friends?[23]

3. "Hate is too great a burden to bear. It injures the hater more than it injures the hated." (Coreta Scott King)[24] She may have a point? For example, "Hunting Blue: the Hatred Continues." Those who don't think as I think certainly seem less content and less happy than me!

4. Martin Luther King, Jr.: "Darkness cannot drive out darkness. Only light can do that. Hate cannot drive out hate; only love can do that."[25] The haters have (demonstrate) so much hate and so little (if any) love!

5. Nelson Mandela, the South African anti-apartheid activist, politition and statesman, served as the first president of South Africa (1994-1999). He was elected in a democratic election, the first black head of state in the country. Most remember Mandela for the time he spent in prison. After twenty-seven years, he was released by F. W. deKlerk in 1990. A Nobel peace Prize winner, he died at the age of 95. (December, 2013)[26]

Though I may not have agreed with everything Mandela did or believed, this quote says a lot about the man, and about hatred. "As I walked out the door toward the gate that would lead to my freedom, I knew if I didn't leave my bitterness and hatred behind, I'd still be in prison." How much happier and free we would be if we could rid our mind and souls of bitterness and hatred that seeks to claim our every day!

6. Echoing others quoted here, Lawana Blackwell's quote equates hatred to a burning coal, a briquette that can burn forever: "The hatred you're carrying is a live coal in your heart-far more damaging to yourself than to them."[27] Blackwell is a well-known writer who has published thirteen novels, many set in the 19th century English countryside. She and her husband live near Dallas .

7. Charles Stanley, the founder of In Touch Ministries, was a Southern Baptist pastor and writer. He was senior pastor of First Baptist Church in Atlanta. His popular radio and television broadcasts are (were) heard around the world in fifty languages. His quote: "God is responsible for the consequences of other's obedience. We are responsible for the consequences of our disobedience."[28]

8. Will Rogers (11-4-1879 to 10-15-1935), the American vaudeville performer, actor, and humorous social commentator, lived at (in) a time different than 2000-2024. A Roger's quote perhaps saw what was to come: "We don't give our criminals much punishment, but we sure give 'em plenty of publicity."[29]

9. Robert Kennedy: "Every society gets the kind of criminal it deserves. What is equally true is that every community gets the kind of law enforcement it insists on."[30]

10. Unknown quote: "Real heroes die serving the law, not resisting it."

And finally: "Everyone knows the "to serve and protect" police motto, but the last part of that says, "without fear or prejudice.""

Consider thoughts from Orwell, Chekhov, Shakespeare, Carnegie, Graham, and Fransis:

"All issues are political issues, and politics in itself is a mass of lies, evasions, folly, hatred, and schizophrenia." George Orwell[31]

"Love, friendship, and respect do not unite people as much as a common hatred for something." Anton Chekhov[32]

"In time we hate which we often fear." William Shakespeare[33]

"Instead of worrying about what people say of you, why not spend time trying to accomplish something we'll observe." Dale Carnegie[34]

"Racial prejudice, anti-Semitism or hatred of anyone with different beliefs have no place in the human mind or heart." Billy Graham[35]

"Lord, make me an instrument of thy peace Where there is hate, let me sow love." Fransis of Assisi[36]

Epilogue

> "Laws are essential to our freedoms."

I'M NOT SURE who said that? Maybe Neill Gorsuch? I like the truth expressed. Consider this:

1. What if there were not speed limits on our streets or roadways? Would you let your kids play or ride bikes there?

2. What if there were no stop signs or stop lights? Would you feel safe driving the streets of your neighborhood or business district?

3. Consider jay walking. What if it was allowed on the streets and highways? Would that hamper your travel, your drive to work, or your rush to the hospital or ER? You might need to replace your horn often!

4. What if there were no laws affecting food preparation, packaging, or sales? Would you trust your family health without question?

5. What if there was no code enforcement for housing or commercial buildings? Would you be okay with a bar, tavern, or late-night club next to your church or child's school? Would you like six outdoor basketball courts between your house and your "next door" neighbor?

6. What if there were no restrictions on admission to movies, casinos, adult entertainment establishments?

7. What if you and others could drive drugged or drunk, without any police to stop and question you?

8. What if there was no restriction on the purchase of firearms, obtaining a driver's license, getting a marriage license, or a pilot's license?

9. What if anyone could be a doctor, nurse, policeman, pharmacist, or even a sports official?

10. What if there were no laws from the beginning? If Moses never came down the mountain with the Ten Commandments? We would not have had the Lone Ranger, Roy Rogers, the Cisco Kid, Perry Mason, Colombo, Peter Gunn, Joe Friday, Clint Eastwood, Kojak, Maverick, or Wyatt Earp; no Rifleman, Bonanza, Untouchables, Hawaii Five O, Law and Order, SVU. Superman, Batman, etc.?

"Hunting Blue: And Hating America" continues with the sequel. "Hunting Blue: The Hatred Continues." The stories are similar, a mix of real people and events, and many fictitious people and events. Readers will recognize names like Alton Sterling (Baton Rouge), George Floyd (Minneapolis), Briana Taylor (Louisville), and Jacob Blake (Kenosha). Each was a central character in actual police settings. Each a national news story for weeks.

You'll have to read the sequel for the stories of Samuel L (Biloxi, MS), Charly Holmes (Berkeley, MO), and Gus and Millie (Jackson, MS). You'll identify with Dominique and Iman (Atlanta), maybe challenge my answer to the question: When Will It Stop? You'll discover new information on Police Shooting Stats. You'll ask yourself: Which stories are real and which are just made-up? That was my plan from the start! I hope you'll purchase and read both.[37]

The Tom Dooley and Mack the Knife Stories

SOME OF THE stories in this book were written five years ago; others in more recent months and weeks. I write, and later review, then maybe rewrite as needed. A story or two might be thrown out, never making the final manuscript. This story was written as an afterthought, just two days before sending it to the publisher. It is not even listed by title among the other forty stories.

Sleepless nights ar common for me. Last night from about eleven until five o'clock this morning, I wrestled with two songs from the 1950s; two characters: Tom Dooley and Mack the Knife. They filled my conscious though silent thinking for five hours in bed, tossing and turning. I have no explanation for that. Stuff like that is not uncommon for me when I write.

Tom Dooley, a real person, was recorded by the Kingston Trio (1958). Mack the Knife, a fictional character from the 1928 music drama, "The Threepenny Opera." Tom Dooley," a North Carolina folk song, recounts the murder of Laura Foster in Wilke's County; the criminal, Tom Dula. His family name is pronounced Dooley in the Dialect of the locals. The most memorable lines of the song are the oft-repeated chorus:

> "Hang down your head Tom Dooley
> Hang down you head and cry
> Hang down your head Tom Dooley
> Poor boy you're bound to die."

Thomas Land is credited as the song writer, a story of love, hate, and murder. (Incidentally, Tom Dula was hanged for his crime).

The first four lines of the lengthy Mack the Knife song might be the most familiar:

"Oh the shark, babe, has such teeth, dear
And it shows them pearly white
Just as Mack the Knife has old MacHeath, babe
And he keeps it out of sight."

Or, "scarlet billiows start to spread, so there's never, never a trace of red."

The song was composed by Kurt Weill; lyrics by Bertolt Brecht. It was first recorded by Louis Armstrong (1955(, but the most popular version was in 1959 by Bobby Darrin. The song recreated a time in the London underworld, a criminal named MacHeath.

Why include these two songs (stories) in "Hunting Blue?"

I was sixteen when, like every other high schooler, we sang and danced with Bobby Darrin on American Bandstand. There were no protests in Carolina when Laura Foster was murdered. The homes and businesses of Wilke's County were not burned to the ground because of Dula's rage. The streets of London were not set ablaze and left in smoke and shambles at the fate and last breaths of Miss Lottie Lenya, Suki Tawdry, and Lucy Brown.

But, that's the point, right? That's why I include these two stories. What happened in Ferguson after the Michael Brown shooting, and in Minneapolis, after the George Floyd shooting, and in Kenosha, after the Jacob Blake shooting, didn't have to happen! Wrongful death suits didn't (don't) have to be filed, as long as justice is served.

Google both songs and listen. So, now, if you didn't know the characters or the songs before, you will know and remember Tom Dooley and his story; Mack the Knife and his story. When you get together with family and friends and talk about the songs of the 1950s, you will be able to amaze everyone with your tremendous knowledge of pop music. Just tell them that Rich provided the background.

Endnotes

1. www.history.com-news

2. Chaparro, Fabiana, Chris Boyette, and Alisha Ebrahimji. "Chicago Reels from Violent Holiday Weekend: More than 100 Shot, 19 Fatally." CNN, July 8, 2024. https://www.cnn.com/2024/07/08/us/chicago-shootings-july-fourth-weekend/index.html.

3. "Rod Smart." Wikipedia, September 11, 2024. https://en.wikipedia.org/wiki/Rod_Smart.

4. "Emmett Till." Wikipedia, September 24, 2024. https://en.wikipedia.org/wiki/Emmett_Till.

5. Scott, Mike. "After Years of Silence, New Orleans Writer Jarvis DeBerry Opens up about His Family's Medical Nightmare." NOLA.com, December 6, 2019. https://www.nola.com/entertainment_life/after-years-of-silence-new-orleans-writer-jarvis-deberry-opens-up-about-his-family-s/article_f86fba68-184d-11ea-813f-3b6764b91126.html.

6. en.wikipedia.org-wiki-jeff sessions

7. "NPR." Wikipedia, August 31, 2024. https://en.wikipedia.org/wiki/NPR.

8. "Killing of Trayvon Martin." Wikipedia, September 17, 2024. https://en.wikipedia.org/wiki/Killing_of_Trayvon_Martin.

9. "What Happened on September 27." History.com. Accessed September 27, 2024. https://www.history.com/this-day-in-history.

10. Enwikipedia.org-wiki- killing-of-Michael Brown

11. Szalai, Jennifer. "Black Lives Matter and the Intrepid Lives That Preceded It." The New York Times, January 24, 2018. https://www.nytimes.com/2018/01/24/books/review-when-they-call-you-terrorist-patrisse-khan-cullors-more-beautiful-terrible-history-jeanne-theoharis.html.

12. Loaded on Feb. 15, 2001 published in Prison Legal News February. " ." Louisiana Abandons Private Juvenile Prisons | Prison Legal News. Accessed October 8, 2024. https://www.prisonlegalnews.org/news/2001/feb/15/louisiana-abandons-private-juvenile-prisons/.

13. "Atlanta Pride." Wikipedia, September 16, 2024. https://en.wikipedia.org/wiki/Atlanta_Pride.

14. "2016 Shooting of Dallas Police Officers." Wikipedia, September 12, 2024. https://en.wikipedia.org/wiki/2016_shooting_of_Dallas_police_officers.

15. "2006 UNC SUV Attack." Wikipedia, August 14, 2024. https://en.wikipedia.org/wiki/2006_UNC_SUV_attack.

16. "2016 Nice Truck Attack." Wikipedia, October 3, 2024. https://en.wikipedia.org/wiki/2016_Nice_truck_attack.

17. "Luis Bracamontes." Wikipedia, June 24, 2024. https://en.wikipedia.org/wiki/Luis_Bracamontes.

18. "Markeith Loyd Sentenced to Death for 2017 Murder of Orlando Police Lt. Debra Clayton." CBS News. Accessed October 8, 2024. https://www.cbsnews.com/news/markeith-loyd-death-sentence-2017-murder-officer-debra-clayton-orlando-police/.

19. Press, The Associated. "An Ohio Police Officer Was Cleared in the Shooting of Teenager Ma'khia Bryant." NPR, March 12, 2022. https://www.npr.org/2022/03/12/1086283433/police-officer-cleared-makhia-bryant-shooting.

20. McMenamin, Dave. "Lebron James Explains Why He Deleted Tweet on Police Shooting of Ma'khia Bryant." ESPN. Accessed October 8, 2024. https://www.espn.com/nba/story/_/id/31306343/lebron-james-explains-why-deleted-tweet-police-shooting-makhia-bryant.

21. Marc Bona, cleveland.com. "9 Things about Rick Monday's U.S. Flag-Saving Incident 40 Years Ago: Flag Day." cleveland, June 14, 2016. https://www.cleveland.com/entertainment/2016/06/9_things_about_rick_mondays_us.html.

22 "A Quote by George Bernard Shaw." Goodreads. Accessed October 2, 2024. https://www.goodreads.com/quotes/113999-hatred-is-the-coward-s-revenge-for-being-intimidated.

23 Johann Wolfgang von Goethe–hatred is something peculiar.... Accessed October 8, 2024. https://www.brainyquote.com/quotes/johann_wolfgang_von_goeth_150550.

24 Coretta Scott King–Hate is too great a burden to bear.... Accessed September 18, 2024. https://www.brainyquote.com/quotes/coretta_scott_king_141009.

25 Martin Luther King, jr.–darkness cannot drive out... Accessed September 18, 2024. https://www.brainyquote.com/quotes/martin_luther_king_jr_101472.

26 "A Quote by Nelson Mandela." Goodreads. Accessed September 19, 2024. https://www.goodreads.com/quotes/278812-as-i-walked-out-the-door-toward-the-gate-that.

27 "A Quote from Catherine's Heart." Goodreads. Accessed October 8, 2024. https://www.goodreads.com/quotes/11740-the-hatred-you-re-carrying-is-a-live-coal-in-your.

28 "Charles F. Stanley Quote: 'God Is Responsible for the Consequences of Our Obedience, We Are Responsible for the Consequences of Our Disobedience.'" Quotefancy. Accessed September 19, 2024. https://quotefancy.com/quote/1426098/Charles-F-Stanley-God-is-responsible-for-the-consequences-of-our-obedience-WE-are.

29 "Will Rogers Quote: 'we Don't Give Our Criminals Much Punishment, but We Sure Give 'em Plenty of Publicity.'" Quotefancy. Accessed September 19, 2024. https://quotefancy.com/quote/933067/Will-Rogers-We-don-t-give-our-criminals-much-punishment-but-we-sure-give-em-plenty-of.

30 Robert Kennedy–every society gets the kind of criminal... Accessed September 19, 2024. https://www.brainyquote.com/quotes/robert_kennedy_400860.

31. "A Quote from All Art Is Propaganda." Goodreads. Accessed October 8, 2024. https://www.goodreads.com/quotes/1292558-all-issues-are-political-issues-and-politics-itself-is-a.

32. "A Quote by Anton Chekhov." Goodreads. Accessed September 19, 2024. https://www.goodreads.com/quotes/7692205-love-friendship-and-respect-do-not-unite-people-as-much.

33. "A Quote from Antony and Cleopatra." Goodreads. Accessed October 8, 2024. https://www.goodreads.com/quotes/40746-in-time-we-hate-that-which-we-often-fear.

34. Dale Carnegie–instead of worrying about what people say... Accessed September 19, 2024. https://www.brainyquote.com/quotes/dale_carnegie_388905.

35. Billy Graham quotes. Accessed September 19, 2024. https://www.brainyquote.com/quotes/billy_graham_626312.

36. "Prayer of St Francis." Science of Mind Spiritual Center Los Angeles. Accessed September 19, 2024. https://somspiritualcenterla.org/prayer-of-st-francis?gad_source=1&gclid=CjwKCAjwl6-3Bh-BWEiwApN6_ksDjEei_84RxY6d79rV6gbD—MhtUg0nqTuX-CNxqvezOf0JwGiHlRoCwEoQAvD_BwE.

37. Korhonen, Veera. "People Shot to Death by U.S. Police, by Race 2024." Statista, September 23, 2024. https://www.statista.com/statistics/585152/people-shot-to-death-by-us-police-by-race/.